Crowdfunding European Business

This book questions the ability of crowdfunding (especially in the lending and equity-based models) to contribute to the development of European businesses and, therefore, to the relaunch of the European economy. Following a mainly micro (firm-based) approach, the study investigates the advantages of crowd investors' increased role in making financial resources available to the industrial base, thus reinvigorating economic growth across the European Union.

The book reframes contemporary issues surrounding corporate finance and develops relevant knowledge to help companies succeed when it comes to securing the means to grow. It provides new and interesting insights into the alternative finance market, in light of the global financial crisis and the COVID-19 pandemic. The book describes the main alternative finance models which include not only lending and equity-based crowdfunding, but also marketplace lending, balance sheet lending, invoice trading, securities, real estate crowdfunding, and profit-sharing. It also analyses the due diligence process and other value-added services provided by platforms and backers. The book outlines a systematic understanding of crowdfunding as a substitute or complement to other forms of entrepreneurial finance and unpacks some of the misunderstandings surrounding the crowdfunding industry and its future evolution. The conclusions reached can be of help to entrepreneurs who have limited knowledge of the crowdfunding tool and the associated benefits.

As such, this book is a valuable resource for students, researchers, professionals, and practitioners interested in discovering or better understanding the crowdfunding process, its characteristics, and the range of players in this market.

Antonella Francesca Cicchiello is a research fellow in Financial Markets and Institutions at the Catholic University of the Sacred Heart, Department of Economic and Social Sciences (DiSES) of Piacenza (Italy).

Routledge Focus on Economics and Finance

The fields of economics are constantly expanding and evolving. This growth presents challenges for readers trying to keep up with the latest important insights. Routledge Focus on Economics and Finance presents short books on the latest big topics, linking in with the most cutting-edge economics research.

Individually, each title in the series provides coverage of a key academic topic, whilst collectively the series forms a comprehensive collection across the whole spectrum of economics.

Economic Innovations
Creating New Instruments to Improve Economic Life
Beth Webster and Bill Scales

Well-being and Growth in Advanced Economies
The Need to Prioritise Human Development
Maurizio Pugno

The Economics of ObamaCare
Łukasz Jasiński

Monetary Policy and Inflation
Quantity Theory of Money
Mateusz Machaj

Customer Data Sharing Frameworks
Twelve Lessons for the World
Anton Didenko, Natalia Jevglevskaja and Ross P. Buckley

Crowdfunding European Business
Antonella Francesca Cicchiello

For more information about this series, please visit: www.routledge.com/ Routledge-Focus-on-Economics-and-Finance/book-series/RFEF

Crowdfunding European Business

Antonella Francesca Cicchiello

Routledge
Taylor & Francis Group

LONDON AND NEW YORK

First published 2024
by Routledge
4 Park Square, Milton Park, Abingdon, Oxon OX14 4RN

and by Routledge
605 Third Avenue, New York, NY 10158

Routledge is an imprint of the Taylor & Francis Group, an informa business

British Library Cataloguing-in-Publication Data
A catalogue record for this book is available from the British Library

Library of Congress Cataloging-in-Publication Data
Names: Cicchiello, Antonella Francesca, author.
Title: Crowdfunding European business / Antonella Francesca Cicchiello.
Description: Abingdon, Oxon ; New York, NY : Routledge, 2024. | Series: Routledge focus on economics and finance | Includes bibliographical references and index.
Identifiers: LCCN 2023055350 (print) | LCCN 2023055351 (ebook) | ISBN 9781032464008 (hardback) | ISBN 9781032464015 (paperback) | ISBN 9781003381518 (ebook)
Subjects: LCSH: Crowd funding--Europe. | Business enterprises--Europe--Finance. | Investments--Europe.
Classification: LCC HG5428 .C53 2024 (print) | LCC HG5428 (ebook) | DDC 332/.04154094--dc23/eng/20231221
LC record available at https://lccn.loc.gov/2023055350
LC ebook record available at https://lccn.loc.gov/2023055351

ISBN: 978-1-032-46400-8 (hbk)
ISBN: 978-1-032-46401-5 (pbk)
ISBN: 978-1-003-38151-8 (ebk)

DOI: 10.4324/9781003381518

Typeset in Times
by MPS Limited, Dehradun

To my husband,
who has walked every step of this journey with me.

Contents

Figures

Tables

Introduction

The main source of financing for European businesses (in some countries more than others) is still bank credit. However, following Basel III and the introduction of the ratings-based approach, it has become increasingly expensive for businesses to obtain capital from banks – both economically and in terms of time. In this context, one of the needs to be addressed is certainly the strengthening of the equity ratio which has a positive impact on the rating and solvency of the company. Another important challenge is to find and use alternative or supplementary forms to bank credit.

Taking this into consideration, this book is intended as a means to reframe contemporary issues surrounding corporate finance and develop relevant knowledge to help companies succeed when it comes to securing the means to grow. Relying on the work of different academics, practitioners, and institutions, this book aims to provide a systematic understanding of crowdfunding as a substitute or complement to other forms of entrepreneurial finance and also to emphasise some misunderstandings surrounding the crowdfunding industry and its future evolution.

The most distinguishable features of this book in its development phase include:

- A section on the evolution of entrepreneurial finance in the light of past and more recent crises as it is useful for understanding the framework within which the crowdfunding industry has developed.
- A key point on how both first-time entrepreneurs and seasoned founders leading high-growth companies should navigate the crowdfunding ecosystem to raise funds successfully.
- A forward-looking perspective on how technological evolution will continue to shape entrepreneurial finance in the future by creating new challenges as well as new opportunities and risks.

Gaining knowledge of alternative financing methods can help both start-up companies and growing businesses raise the capital they need to be

DOI: 10.4324/9781003381518-1

successful and provide the flexibility they need to adapt to a demanding and changing market. Democratising entrepreneurial finance is certainly useful because it can induce a transfusion of new resources and ideas, but the peculiarities of the crowdfunding market and the questions regarding its contribution to businesses' scalability should not be forgotten.

The book is organised as follows. Chapter 1 opens with a detailed picture of the changing landscape of the European entrepreneurial finance market. It details the meaning of the alternative finance market and its evolution over time, further outlining the new business models, their functioning, and their operation and characteristics. Finally, the chapter identifies the risks arising from the transformation of entrepreneurial finance. Chapter 2 concerns equity-based crowdfunding, which is one of the three investment models of the capital-raising alternative finance ecosystem. More precisely, it explains the funding mechanisms in equity crowdfunding and the platforms' design. Then, the chapter provides an insight into the regulation of equity-based crowdfunding in Europe, both nationally and supranationally, and the tax relief offered to investors and businesses. The chapter concludes with an overview of the key players in the European equity crowdfunding market. Chapter 3 deals with the other model of the capital-raising alternative finance ecosystem, that of loan-based crowdfunding. It provides a detailed description of the lending process and platforms business models. Then, it examines the European regulatory context and reviews the characteristics of the tax incentives available for this type of crowdfunding in France, the UK, and Belgium (the only countries that adopt tax incentives to encourage lending-based crowdfunding). The chapter concludes by identifying the main players in the P2P business lending market. Chapter 4 examines the impact of crowdfunding on the growth opportunities of European businesses. The first part of the chapter analyses the due diligence process and other value-added services, as well as the potential benefits provided by backers beyond the provision of financial resources in order to stimulate the value co-creation process. In particular, this part of the chapter addresses the thorny question of whether the growth of crowdfunding-backed firms is linked to the ability of platforms to select companies through an effective due diligence process – that allows them to screen lower-quality or fraudulent projects and mitigate information asymmetries between project creators and funders – or to the value created by the crowd during the investment process. The second part of the chapter deals with the issue of the impact of crowdfunding investments on target companies by examining the results of research conducted by trade associations and coming from the academic sphere. Relying on these studies, the chapter aims to provide an exhaustive answer to a question that has long been linked to crowdfunding investment, such as the existence of a causal connection between crowdfunding financing and the growth of backed firms. Chapter 5 investigates the positive impact of crowdfunding on the cultural and creative industries and female entrepreneurs' empowerment, as well as its role in the transition towards a circular economy. Chapter 6 concludes the book with some final reflections on the consequential future in the ongoing evolution of the alternative finance market in Europe. This final part of the book is intended to outline three main points: lessons from the past, outlook on the future of alternative finance, and questions still to be answered.

1 The funding gap issue and the landscape of alternative finance

1.1 Financing entrepreneurship in times of crisis: From the 2007–2009 global financial crisis to the COVID-19 pandemic

The European entrepreneurial finance landscape has changed dramatically over the last two decades. The Global Financial Crisis (2008–2009), due to problems in the subprime mortgage market, and the subsequent European sovereign debt crisis (2012–2013) led to a tightening of credit conditions, raising concerns about the ability of businesses (and especially micro, small, and medium-sized enterprises) to access traditional bank financing (Brunnermeier, 2009; Campello *et al.*, 2010). The shock of credit rationing in the loan market has increased the demand for alternative forms of external finance by financially constrained firms (i.e., firms whose loan applications were rejected outright) and self-rationing firms (i.e., firms that rejected loans or did not apply for loans due to high costs) (Casey and O'Toole, 2014). However, the increase in demand and usage by firms of alternative forms of financing was not only the consequence of bank lending constraints in times of crisis. The growing evolution in information and communication technologies (ICT), as well as changes in regulation, has modified the playing field for traditional banks and financial institutions, favouring the appearance of new competitors and new forms of competition in the financial services industry (Bruton *et al.*, 2015). In the meantime, the rapid proliferation of new financial companies based on technological platforms, known as FinTechs, has brought new ways and approaches to banking from both the supply and demand sides (Thakor, 2020). On the supply side, the use of information technology has enabled new specialised entrants to provide lower-cost, customised, and non-intermediated financial products and services designed to meet customers' evolving preferences. On the demand side, disruptive technological innovations such as artificial intelligence (AI), big data analytics, blockchain, and distributed ledger technology (DLT) have changed the way

DOI: 10.4324/9781003381518-2

financial products and services are structured, delivered, and consumed, transforming customer behaviours and preferences.

In this evolving context, many new players (such as incubators, accelerators, crowdfunding platforms, family offices, and more) have emerged in the entrepreneurial finance landscape, creating new opportunities for entrepreneurs and businesses to raise capital beyond the traditional forms of financing (Block *et al.*, 2018). These new players have given early-stage ventures and SMEs alternative options to raise capital and the opportunity to finance their businesses with more flexible and customised fundraising strategies and instruments (Bellavitis *et al.*, 2017). At the same time, by harnessing the power of the internet, these new players have allowed many innovative businesses from both developed and emerging countries to bridge geographical distances and attract investors located in different countries, thus alleviating their financing difficulties.

In the first quarter of 2020, the entire world was hit by an unprecedented health crisis due to the novel Corona Virus Disease (later named 'COVID-19'). Initially reported in the city of Wuhan, China, in December 2019, the virus then spread to other provinces in mainland China and neighbouring countries like Thailand, South Korea, Japan, and Singapore, quickly turning into a global pandemic, as declared by the World Health Organisation (WHO) on 30 January 2020. In Europe, Italy was the first country affected by the health emergency. Starting as a health crisis, the coronavirus pandemic soon transformed into an unprecedented social and economic crisis with consequences far worse than the 2008–2009 Global Financial Crisis. The pandemic and the effects of the lockdown measures to contain the spread of the virus have produced severe damage to the real economy and extraordinary volatility in the financial markets around the world. In addition to the massive loss of human lives, the pandemic has worsened people's well-being and mental health (Brodeur *et al.*, 2021), reduced agricultural production, food security, and livelihoods (Workie *et al.*, 2020), and caused disruptions in transportation services, supply chains, and markets, with severe consequences for workers, their families, and businesses. The pandemic also resulted in a reduction in the global supply of bank credit, especially in more affected countries (Çolak and Öztekin, 2021). Unlike the global financial crisis, during which banks significantly cut the supply of loans to non-financial firms and charged higher interest rates (Brunnermeier, 2009), at the onset of the pandemic, an influx of funds from liquidity injection programs and depositors, together with loan guarantee programs and other forms of credit support for businesses, has enabled banks to cope with the surge in demand for liquidity (Li *et al.*, 2020). However, in the months following the outbreak of the pandemic, despite government stimulus and liquidity injection measures aimed at avoiding credit supply disruptions, banks have tightened lending standards following spikes in borrowers' credit risk and greater risk aversion due to the worsening of the economic outlook. This has led to higher interest rates, smaller loans approved than requested, and the demand for more collateral (Çolak and Öztekin, 2021). In this context of uncertainty context, the online alternative finance industry has demonstrated its resilience to the challenges of the COVID-19 pandemic, maintaining its growth in most markets while showing its ability to realign with emerging needs and conditions.

1.2   The European alternative finance market: Growth and development at both regional and national levels

The online alternative finance market has expanded significantly around Europe (including the United Kingdom) in recent years, growing from $1.5 billion in 2013 to $23.2 billion in 2019 (Ziegler *et al.*, 2021). Despite a drop in the overall market volume in 2020 due to the COVID-19 pandemic and Brexit, the market volume reported for 2020 ($22.6 billion) remained higher than that reported in 2018 ($18.1 billion). Figure 1.1 shows the European online alternative finance market volumes from 2013 to 2020.

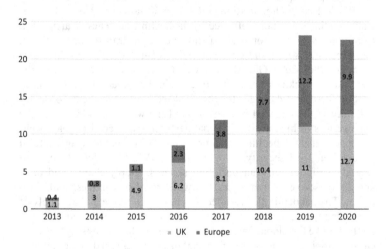

Figure 1.1 European online alternative finance market volumes 2013–2020, in USD billions.

Source: Author's elaboration on data from Ziegler *et al.* (2021).

Note: According to Ziegler *et al.* (2021), the European Online Alternative Finance Market Europe is intended to include the entire geographical Europe.

At a country level, the United Kingdom continues to be the heart of the development and growth of online alternative finance, accounting for 56% of the European market in terms of volume. The UK online alternative finance market has shown enormous resilience during the COVID-19 pandemic, growing from $11 billion in 2019 to $12.6 billion in 2020. Excluding the United Kingdom, the countries that have shown the highest growth rates from 2019 to 2020 are Germany ($1.42 billion to $1.48 billion), France ($1.32 billion to $1.66 billion), and Italy ($1.55 billion to $1.86 billion). Figure 1.2 shows the regional alternative finance market volumes in 2020.

The alternative finance market has taken on a key role in creating a more inclusive financial system during the emergency situation due to the pandemic, helping European micro, small, and medium-sized enterprises (MSMEs) to withstand the devastating impact of economic lockdowns. According to Ziegler *et al.* (2021), in 2019, the volume of online alternative finance attributed to European MSMEs was $4.3 billion, and in 2020 it increased further to $5.2 billion. It is worth highlighting that 34% of these funds were raised by female entrepreneurs. Alternative financial markets represent an increasingly important driver of growth in emerging and

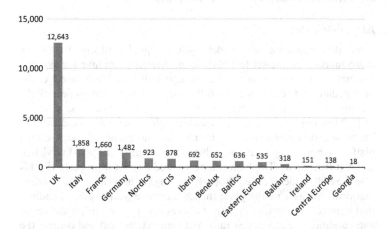

Figure 1.2 Regional alternative finance volumes 2020 in USD millions.

Source: Author's elaboration on data from Ziegler *et al.* (2021).

Note: The Baltic market encompasses alternative finance in Estonia, Latvia, and Lithuania. Central Europe consists of three countries: Austria, Switzerland, and Liechtenstein. Iberia includes Portugal and Spain. The Benelux market includes Belgium, the Netherlands, and Luxembourg. The Nordic market includes Denmark, Finland, Iceland, Norway, and Sweden. CIS (Commonwealth of Independent States) includes Armenia, Belarus, Kazakhstan, Kyrgyzstan, Russia, and Tajikistan.

developing economies, helping successful businesses attract international investors outside of traditional global financial centres.

Traditional financial institutions such as banks, investment funds, private equity firms, and insurance companies are playing an increasingly important role in the functioning of the online alternative finance market. Traditional financial institutions either collaborate with platforms by co-financing investments and loans or operate their own platforms.

1.3   The main alternative finance models

The alternative finance ecosystem comprises all those entrepreneurial financing instruments, channels, and systems developed outside the traditional and established financial markets and whose objective is to cover the funding gaps faced by young innovative businesses and SMEs. Over the last two decades, technological innovation has allowed the alternative finance ecosystem to develop significantly, including increasingly advanced financing models which, through online platforms, connect individuals, businesses, and other entities seeking funds with a vast network of retail and professional investors. The alternative finance models can be divided into investment models (debt and equity) and non-investment models (Ziegler *et al.*, 2021).

1.3.1   Debt models

Alternative financing debt models include digital platforms that allow individuals or businesses to obtain loans directly from investors via the internet. Debt models represent an alternative to bank-based credit intermediation and include the following activities: peer-to-peer (P2P) lending, balance sheet lending, invoice trading, and securities.

P2P lending is a form of financial technology that allows individuals, businesses, or other entities to borrow or lend money through online platforms bypassing banks or other financial institutions (Havrylchyk and Verdier, 2018). The loan can be secured against a property (in this case the P2P model is called Property lending) or unsecured. P2P lending platforms act as a marketplace (hence the name Marketplace Lending) that connects borrowers directly to investors; they establish the terms and conditions (e.g., interest rates and transaction fees) and control the transactions. Depending on whether the borrower is an individual or a business, the P2P lending model is referred to as Consumer Lending or Business Lending. The P2P lending model is also known as social lending, crowd lending, loan-based crowdfunding, and marketplace lending. For further information, please refer to Chapter 3.

In the balance sheet lending model, the lender is not a peer-to-peer investor but the platform itself that lends money directly to a consumer or business borrower. The granted loans (secured against a property or unsecured) are therefore entered on the balance sheet of the platform which assumes the entire credit risk. Also known as portfolio lending, this model is similar to that of traditional bank lending and usually requires the platform to have a banking license.

Mainly used in supply-chain finance activities, the invoice exchange model connects businesses – which due to cash flow problems want to sell their outstanding invoices or receivables at a discount – with private or institutional investors looking for short-term investments. Typically, the investors pre-finance the full-face value of the invoice or fractions of it (the so-called advance) and receive in exchange the advance value and all accrued interest upon maturity. The investors do not resume the credit risk for a potential default of the invoice (i.e., in the event that both the debtor and the selling company are unable to fully repay the invoice amount plus the accrued interest). The digital platform acts as a trusted intermediary, verifying the invoice and the seller's creditworthiness. It also establishes the interest rate on the face value of the invoice as well as the percentage funded using an internal risk-based pricing mechanism (for more information, see Dorfleitner *et al.*, 2017).

Finally, the debt-based securities model allows private or institutional investors to purchase bonds, debentures, or mini-bonds, issued by a company (generally a small and medium-sized enterprises) in exchange for a predetermined amount of interest payments, along with the return of the principal upon the bond's maturity date.

1.3.2 Investment models

Investment models include digital platforms that allow individuals or institutional funders to purchase unlisted shares or securities issued by a company, usually a start-up or SME. Equity-based crowdfunding (which will be discussed in detail in Chapter 2) is the most popular model and has built a solid reputation over the last decade. It represents an alternative and less regulated way of raising public equity compared to traditional stock exchanges. Companies undergoing an equity crowd-funding campaign make an open offer on a registered platform, listing the amount they are seeking to raise and the percentage of equity offered. On the other side of the process, a diversified group of crowd investors subscribe to ordinary shares (with or without voting and pre-emption rights), becoming minority shareholders and expecting financial returns on their investments in terms of capital distributions and dividends (Cumming *et al.*, 2019).

Real estate crowdfunding represents a recently introduced subset of the equity-based model. It allows retail and institutional investors to finance entrepreneurial projects related to the real estate industry by subscribing to unlisted equity shares of the company that owns the entrepreneurial project (Montgomery *et al.*, 2018). In exchange for their capital, investors receive a monthly rent or, in the most frequent cases, a capital gain on the sale of the property. Real estate investment opportunities typically include newly built or existing residential and commercial properties and infrastructures that are sold or rented, in some cases after being renovated. Investment opportunities can also include the so-called 'greenfield projects', i.e., ex novo projects, which start from non-urbanised areas (usually agricultural). Real estate projects are usually financed only to a minority extent through crowdfunding while the largest part is represented by bank credit and self-financing. To promote investment liquidity, real estate platforms can implement a secondary market where investors buy and sell shares.

Another interesting variant of equity-focused models is profit-sharing crowdfunding (Belleflamme *et al.*, 2014). In the profit-sharing scheme, retail and institutional investors purchase securities from a company in exchange for a share of future profits or royalties of the business (De Buysere *et al.*, 2012).

1.3.3   Non-investment models

Non-investment-based models include donation-based and reward-based crowdfunding. Donation-based crowdfunding has its origins in the most ancient tradition of patronage. For centuries, in fact, noble and bourgeois families, endowed with a high economic availability, promoted and financially supported the artistic and cultural activity of artists and writers, also providing for their material needs. The internet and technological advances have brought charitable fundraising out of the aristocratic social circles and into modern web-enabled crowd-funding platforms, allowing everyone, from anywhere in the world to contribute to specific causes. Donation-based crowdfunding platforms allow donors to provide small funding increments to individuals, projects, or businesses as an act of charity. Donations are mostly given anonymously from individuals with little, if any, social connection to fund seekers (Agrawal *et al.*, 2015). Charitable donors on crowdfunding platforms are mostly motivated by the sense of satisfaction in contributing to specific causes that they consider important and are passionate about (Gleasure and Feller, 2016; Bagheri *et al.*, 2019).

Reward-based crowdfunding is probably the most popular model. It allows individuals and businesses to raise funds from a large audience of crowd investors in return for a non-monetary reward proportional to the amount raised. Businesses or entrepreneurs wishing to bring a new product or service to market can offer a prototype as a reward in exchange for the capital needed for its development or production, as well as feedback from contributors that will be incorporated into design and marketing processes. In this case, the reward model is used as a pre-sales action to test the intended product or service before it is manufactured and available on the market (Mollick, 2014). Pre-sale campaigns help entrepreneurs test the market by identifying consumer preferences in terms of design, feature inclusion, and pricing without committing to the upfront manufacturing, distribution, and marketing costs required to commercialise a new product or service.

1.4 The perceived risks of alternative finance

While alternative financing can provide businesses, especially SMEs, with quick, flexible, and easy access to capital when traditional sources are unavailable, it is important to recognise that this type of financing is not without risks (Farag and Johan, 2021). On the side of fundraisers (i.e., companies and individuals collecting money via online platforms) the risks are mainly related to the lack of protection of intellectual property rights and plagiarism (Valanciene and Jegeleviciute, 2013). In order to obtain funds through an online platform, fundraisers might have to disclose information about a new product and the innovative idea behind it. Under patent law in most European jurisdictions, sharing a product that has not yet been patented qualifies as public disclosure. Such disclosure to the public may constitute, in the absence of a confidentiality or non-disclosure agreement (as in the case of online platforms), an obstacle to the future patenting of the product as it eliminates the element of novelty. According to the US patent law (i.e., the Patent Act), from the moment a patentable idea is disclosed, the inventor has one year to file a patent application. After this period of time, it will not be possible to file a patent on the disclosed product, and the inventor will lose all intellectual property rights. Fundraisers are often unaware of this legislation and allow the deadline to lapse, giving unethical internet users the opportunity to file a patent application first and grab ownership of the idea. Disclosing an original idea on an online platform before filing a patent application can also lead to the risk of plagiarism or illegal imitation by competitors or other experts in the field. Plagiarism risk may reduce fundraisers' willingness to disclose information or even completely discourage the use of alternative financing sources (Wang *et al.*, 2018). It is therefore of fundamental importance to file a patent application before starting a fundraising campaign on an online platform. This prevents the new product from being copied by competitors and made ineligible for registration at the patent office. Another risk associated with alternative financing, and in particular with debt-based models, is represented by the over indebtedness of fundraisers and their inability to fully and promptly cover the borrowed capital. Fundraisers could potentially borrow too large sums and then not be able to repay them, resulting in penalties and damage to their credit rating, as well as greater vulnerability to shocks. Additionally, alternative financing can come with shorter repayment periods and higher interest rates than traditional credit institutions, making it difficult for businesses to manage cash flows (Lenz, 2016). However, this risk can be mitigated by ensuring that the overall cost of the debt capital is adequate in terms of interest rates and maturity for the company's needs. Finally, in the case of investment-based models, fundraisers could set funding targets that are too high and not be able to balance the single (and not continuous) flow of liquidity collected through online platforms with the expenditure needs of the current management of their entrepreneurial activity.

On the investors' side (retail and institutional), there is a number of risks that may demotivate them from engaging in alternative financing (Yasar, 2021). First of all, there is the risk of fraud and fake campaigns created by ill-intentioned users who try to obtain a return from well-intentioned investors (Cumming *et al.*, 2021). An intrinsic characteristic of alternative financing channels is information asymmetry since fundraisers (entrepreneurs and borrowers) hold quantitatively and/or qualitatively more information than the potential investors (Mollick, 2014; Ahlers *et al.*, 2015). This means that investors typically lack all the information they need to adequately analyse the risks and potential returns of their investments and, as a result, make an informed decision. Information asymmetries expose investors to the risk of fraudulent behaviour by fundraisers who can lie about the quality of the project, hide their actual financial position, collect money for counterfeit and fraudulent companies, or use the funds raised for purposes other than those declared, including criminal purposes (Strausz, 2017). Other risks (although rare in European countries) associated with alternative financing channels are money laundering and misuse of customer data. In the first case, ill-intentioned investors use the online platform as a cover to transfer illegally acquired money to a shell company created by ill-intentioned fundraisers (Stack *et al.*, 2017). The risk of misuse of customer data comes directly as a consequence of the internet-based nature of alternative financing channels that use online platforms to conduct financial transactions (Shneor and Torjesen, 2020). Data misuse occurs when legitimately collected information is used in a way that goes beyond its original purpose. In the most severe cases, it takes the form of identity theft, i.e., someone steals the personal or financial information of another person and uses it to commit fraud, such as making unauthorised transactions or purchases. It can also consist of data commingling, i.e., data acquired for a specific stated purpose is reused for different purposes or shared with other companies without consent and/or knowledge of the users (Wang, 2023).

Default risk is a particularly relevant part of alternative financing. In the case of non-investment models, and in particular reward-based crowdfunding, there is no guarantee that the product and/or the service will actually be developed and delivered as promised during the campaign. In many cases, investors face delays in delivery (Appio *et al.*, 2020), cancellations (Cumming *et al.*, 2021), or exposure to poor-value products (Mollick and Kuppuswamy, 2014). In the case of debt-based models, borrowers (individuals or companies) are not always able to repay their loans, bonds, debentures, or mini-bonds, exposing lenders to default risk (which is also named credit risk of loans) (Bao *et al.*, 2023). Although online lending platforms apply credit assessment instruments, the presence of information asymmetries makes it difficult to evaluate the authenticity of the information provided by borrowers, compromising the quality of the evaluation (Liu *et al.*, 2019). Furthermore, unlike traditional financing channels, alternative lenders do not accept collateral for their loans. This prevents lenders from accessing the borrower's assets in the event of default. Furthermore, the probability of recovering outstanding debts is very low and costly in case of borrower default.

The risk of default is higher in investment models (such as equity-based crowdfunding) as they involve an investment decision with the prospect of a potential financial return that may result in the loss of entire capital for investors (Reichenbach and Walther, 2021). The main factor that exposes investors to the risk of default is that the companies that usually raise equity capital through online platforms are start-ups – with a high probability of failure within the first five years – and early-stage businesses – whose returns, if any, are highly variable, not guaranteed, and may take several years to materialise. Investing in start-ups and early-stage businesses also involves other risks, including illiquidity, unlikely or infrequent dividends, and possibility of dilution.

The risk of illiquidity is an important risk of alternative financing, as are the limited exit opportunities available to investors. Unlike traditional financial markets where investors can execute a trade or liquidate their position immediately, buying or selling a stock or converting it into cash can be extremely difficult when dealing with alternative financial markets. The inability to liquidate or realise their investments exposes investors to the risk of suffering capital losses even if the company in which they have invested has prospered. It is therefore vital that investors know they have few exit options available to them. These include (i) initial public offerings (IPO), in which the company goes public by selling its shares to the public; (ii) acquisition exit, in the event that the entire company is sold to third parties; (iii) secondary sale, in which the individual investor's shares are sold to a third party; (iv) share buyback, in which the investors' shares are reabsorbed by the company itself; (v) share redemptions, in which the company requires investors to sell a portion of their shares back to the company; and (vi) liquidation of the company, in which the company's assets are sold to pay back creditors and other liabilities. Over the last few years, a number of initiatives have been taken to develop secondary markets for alternative investment where investors can buy and sell shares (Lukkarinen and Schwienbacher, 2023). Nevertheless, to date, only a few platforms provide a secondary market to their investors, and the lack of viable exit opportunities remains a missing point of both equity and debt alternative financing models (Cummings *et al.*, 2020).

With regard to the possibility of dilution, it can occur if the company decides to raise additional capital in the future by issuing new shares (Kleinert and Volkmann, 2019). This comes at the expense of existing shareholders as their percentage ownership of the company will be diluted by the newly issued shared. To protect investors from dilution, some companies offer shares containing pre-emptive rights that give existing shareholders the chance to acquire extra shares during a subsequent fundraising round before those shares are offered to third parties. In this way, existing shareholders can preserve their shareholding, even if new shares are issued.

Finally, it is worth underlining that when investing in start-ups or early-stage businesses the possibility of receiving dividends is quite unlikely. Early-stage businesses usually generate only small, if any, returns and even if they are successful and manage to generate significant returns, these are not distributed to shareholders but reinvested in the business to support its further growth. Any investment returns may take several years to materialise and vary in amount, frequency, and timing.

References

Agrawal, A., Catalini, C., & Goldfarb, A. (2015). Crowdfunding: Geography, social networks, and the timing of investment decisions. *Journal of Economics & Management Strategy*, 24(2), 253–274. 10.1111/jems.12093.

Ahlers, G. K., Cumming, D., Günther, C., & Schweizer, D. (2015). Signaling in equity crowdfunding. *Entrepreneurship Theory and Practice*, 39(4), 955–980. 10.1111/etap.12157.

Appio, F. P., Leone, D., Platania, F., & Schiavone, F. (2020). Why are rewards not delivered on time in rewards-based crowdfunding campaigns? An empirical exploration. *Technological Forecasting and Social Change*, 157, 120069. 10.1016/j.techfore.2020.120069.

Bagheri, A., Chitsazan, H., & Ebrahimi, A. (2019). Crowdfunding motivations: A focus on donors' perspectives. *Technological Forecasting and Social Change*, 146, 218–232. 10.1016/j.techfore.2019.05.002.

Bao, T., Ding, Y., Gopal, R., & Möhlmann, M. (2023). Throwing good money after bad: Risk mitigation strategies in the P2P lending platforms. *Information Systems Frontiers*, 1–21. 10.1007/s10796-023-10423-4.

Bellavitis, C., Filatotchev, I., Kamuriwo, D. S., & Vanacker, T. (2017). Entrepreneurial finance: New frontiers of research and practice: Editorial for the special issue embracing entrepreneurial funding innovations. *Venture Capital*, 19(1–2), 1–16. 10.1080/13691066.2016.1259733.

Belleflamme, P., Lambert, T., & Schwienbacher, A. (2014). Crowdfunding: Tapping the right crowd. *Journal of Business Venturing*, 29(5), 585–609. 10.1016/j.jbusvent.2013.07.003.

Block, J. H., Colombo, M. G., Cumming, D. J., & Vismara, S. (2018). New players in entrepreneurial finance and why they are there. *Small Business Economics*, 50, 239–250. 10.1007/s11187-016-9826-6.

Brodeur, A., Clark, A. E., Fleche, S., & Powdthavee, N. (2021). COVID-19, lockdowns and well-being: Evidence from google trends. *Journal of Public Economics*, 193, 104346. 10.1016/j.jpubeco.2020.104346.

Brunnermeier, M. K. (2009). Deciphering the liquidity and credit crunch 2007–2008. *Journal of Economic Perspectives*, 23(1), 77–100. 10.1257/jep.23.1.77.

Bruton, G., Khavul, S., Siegel, D., & Wright, M. (2015). New financial alternatives in seeding entrepreneurship: Microfinance, crowdfunding, and peer–to–peer innovations. *Entrepreneurship Theory and Practice*, 39(1), 9–26. 10.1111/etap.12143.

Campello, M., Graham, J. R., & Harvey, C. R. (2010). The real effects of financial constraints: Evidence from a financial crisis. *Journal of Financial Economics*, 97(3), 470–487. 10.1016/j.jfineco.2010.02.009.

Casey, E., & O'Toole, C. M. (2014). Bank lending constraints, trade credit and alternative financing during the financial crisis: Evidence from European SMEs. *Journal of Corporate Finance*, 27, 173–193. 10.1016/j.jcorpfin.2014.05.001.

Çolak, G., & Öztekin, Ö. (2021). The impact of COVID-19 pandemic on bank lending around the world. *Journal of Banking & Finance*, 133, 106207. 10.1016/j.jbankfin.2021.106207.

Cumming, D., Hornuf, L., Karami, M., & Schweizer, D. (2021). Disentangling crowdfunding from fraudfunding. *Journal of Business Ethics*, 1–26. 10.1007/s1 0551-021-04942-w.

Cumming, D., Meoli, M., & Vismara, S. (2019). Investors' choices between cash and voting rights: Evidence from dual-class equity crowdfunding. *Research Policy*, 48(8), 103740. 10.1016/j.respol.2019.01.014.

Cummings, M. E., Rawhouser, H., Vismara, S., & Hamilton, E. L. (2020). An equity crowdfunding research agenda: Evidence from stakeholder participation in the rulemaking process. *Small Business Economics*, 54, 907–932. 10.1007/ s11187-018-00134-5.

De Buysere, K., Gajda, O., Kleverlaan, R., Marom, D., & Klaes, M. (2012). A framework for European crowdfunding. Available at: http://www. europecrowdfunding.org/files/2013/06/FRAMEWORK_EU_CROWDFUND-ING.pdf (Retrieved on 25 September 2023).

Dorfleitner, G., Rad, J., & Weber, M. (2017). Pricing in the online invoice trading market: First empirical evidence. *Economics Letters*, 161, 56–61. 10.1016/ j.econlet.2017.09.020.

Farag, H., & Johan, S. (2021). How alternative finance informs central themes in corporate finance. *Journal of Corporate Finance*, 67, 101879. 10.1016/ j.jcorpfin.2020.101879.

Gleasure, R., & Feller, J. (2016). Does heart or head rule donor behaviors in charitable crowdfunding markets? *International Journal of Electronic Commerce*, 20(4), 499–524. 10.1080/10864415.2016.1171975.

Havrylchyk, O., & Verdier, M. (2018). The financial intermediation role of the P2P lending platforms. *Comparative Economic Studies*, 60(1), 115–130. 10.105 7/s41294-017-0045-1.

Lenz, R. (2016). Peer-to-peer lending: Opportunities and risks. *European Journal of Risk Regulation*, 7(4), 688–700. 10.1017/S1867299X00010126.

Li, L., Strahan, P. E., & Zhang, S. (2020). Banks as lenders of first resort: Evidence from the COVID-19 crisis. *The Review of Corporate Finance Studies*, 9(3), 472–500. 10.1093/rcfs/cfaa009.

Liu, H., Qiao, H., Wang, S., & Li, Y. (2019). Platform competition in peer-to-peer lending considering risk control ability. *European Journal of Operational Research*, 274(1), 280–290. 10.1016/j.ejor.2018.09.024.

Kleinert, S., & Volkmann, C. (2019). Equity crowdfunding and the role of investor discussion boards. *Venture Capital*, 21(4), 327–352. 10.1080/13691 066.2019.1569853.

Lukkarinen, A., & Schwienbacher, A. (2023). Secondary market listings in equity crowdfunding: The missing link? *Research Policy*, 52(1), 104648. 10.1016/j.respol.2022.104648.

Mollick, E. (2014). The dynamics of crowdfunding: An exploratory study. *Journal of Business Venturing*, 29(1), 1–16. 10.1016/j.jbusvent.2013.06.005.

Mollick, E. R., & Kuppuswamy, V. (2014). After the campaign: Outcomes of crowdfunding. UNC Kenan-Flagler Research Paper No. 2376997. 10.2139/ssrn.2376997.

Montgomery, N., Squires, G., & Syed, I. (2018). Disruptive potential of real estate crowdfunding in the real estate project finance industry: A literature review. *Property Management*, 36(5), 597–619. 10.1108/PM-04-2018-0032.

Reichenbach, F., & Walther, M. (2021). Signals in equity-based crowdfunding and risk of failure. *Financial Innovation*, 7(1), 1–30. 10.1186/s40854-021-00270-0.

Shneor, R., & Torjesen, S. (2020). Ethical considerations in crowdfunding. In R. Shneor, L. Zhao, & B. T. Flåten (eds.) *Advances in Crowdfunding: Research and Practice* (pp. 161–182). Cham: Palgrave Macmillan. 10.1007/978-3-030-46309-0_8.

Stack, P., Feller, J., O'Reilly, P., Gleasure, R., Li, S., & Cristoforo, J. (2017). Managing risk in business centric crowdfunding platforms. In Proceedings of the 13th International Symposium on Open Collaboration (Article No: 24, pp. 1–4). 10.1145/3125433.3125460.

Strausz, R. (2017). A theory of crowdfunding: A mechanism design approach with demand uncertainty and moral hazard. *American Economic Review*, 107(6), 1430–1476. 10.1257/aer.20151700.

Thakor, A. V. (2020). Fintech and banking: What do we know? *Journal of Financial Intermediation*, 41, 100833. 10.1016/j.jfi.2019.100833.

Valanciene, L., & Jegeleviciute, S. (2013). Valuation of crowdfunding: Benefits and drawbacks. *Economics and Management*, 18(1), 39-48. 10.5755/j01.em.18.1.3713.

Wang, L. (2023). Ethical challenges of data commingling in business. *Frontiers in Business, Economics and Management*, 11(1), 77–79. 10.54097/fbem.v11i1.11768.

Wang, T., Liu, X., Kang, M., & Zheng, H. (2018). Exploring the determinants of fundraisers' voluntary information disclosure on crowdfunding platforms: A risk-perception perspective. *Online Information Review*, 42(3), 324–342. 10.1108/OIR-11-2016-0329.

Workie, E., Mackolil, J., Nyika, J., & Ramadas, S. (2020). Deciphering the impact of COVID-19 pandemic on food security, agriculture, and livelihoods: A review of the evidence from developing countries. *Current Research in Environmental Sustainability*, 2, 100014. 10.1016/j.crsust.2020.100014.

Yasar, B. (2021). The new investment landscape: Equity crowdfunding. *Central Bank Review*, 21(1), 1–16. 10.1016/j.cbrev.2021.01.001.

Ziegler, T., Shneor, R., Wenzlaff, K., Suresh, K., Paes, F. F. D. C., Mammadova, L., … & Knaup, C. (2021). *The 2nd global alternative finance market benchmarking report*. Cambridge Centre for Alternative Finance. Available at: https://www.jbs.cam.ac.uk/faculty-research/centres/alternative-finance/publications/the-2nd-global-alternative-finance-market-benchmarking-report/ (Retrieved on 18 January 2023).

2 Equity-based crowdfunding

The new landscape of entrepreneurial finance

2.1 Introduction

Equity crowdfunding, also referred to as investment-based crowd-funding, crowdinvesting, and securities crowdfunding, is an alternative relatively new source of external equity finance (Vulkan *et al.*, 2016). It targets innovative early-stage ventures that, due to the great uncertainty surrounding them, have limited access to conventional sources of external equity finance such as venture capital and angel finance.

In this type of crowdfunding, investors become shareholders by investing in an early-stage unlisted company in exchange for shares in this company. Investors can expect returns on their investments in the form of dividends from annual profits and pay-outs in case the company launches an Initial Public Offering (IPO) or gets acquired. Some equity crowdfunding platforms allow investors to sell previously purchased shares or advertise their interest in buying shares through secondary markets developed by the platform itself. Secondary markets are usually reserved for platform members and only allow to trade investments in companies that have used the platform to raise funds. Equity crowdfunding offers companies several benefits including access to a broader pool of potential investors, the retention of company control, greater diversification of capital sources, and the possibility of raising funds more quickly. Over the last few years, equity crowdfunding has proved its ability to close funding gaps affecting start-ups and high-tech ventures, establishing itself as a new player in entrepreneurial finance (Block *et al.*, 2018).

2.2 How it works

Equity crowdfunding differs profoundly from other types of this new form of finance for young entrepreneurial companies, namely donation, reward, and lending-based crowdfunding (Schwienbacher and Larralde, 2010). In equity crowdfunding, investors purchase equity or equity-like shares in a company, expecting in return for their funding a financial

DOI: 10.4324/9781003381518-3

compensation that consists of the set of property and administrative rights that arise from the participation in the company.

Depending on the jurisdiction, the platforms allow companies involved in an equity crowdfunding campaign to offer investors different types of financial contracts. In addition to ordinary shares (with or without voting and pre-emptive rights), on some platforms investors can subscribe to convertible bonds, simple agreements for future equity (SAFEs), and silent partnerships. In Germany, companies mostly offer investments in the form of subordinated profit-participating loans (PPLs): hybrid securities that allow greater contractual freedom (Hornuf *et al.*, 2018).

Equity-based crowdfunding usually works according to the 'All-Or-Nothing' (AON) model (Mollick, 2014); thus, a project is considered successfully completed when the capital raising goal is reached or exceeded within the period of time provided by the platform (the latter case is called 'overfunding'). If the equity crowdfunding campaign ends successfully, the invested amounts are automatically transferred from the escrow account to the company account. From this moment the investors officially become shareholders of the company and acquire all established rights. In the event that the funding goal of the campaign is not achieved, all the invested amounts are returned back to the investors. In contrast, in the 'Keep-It-All' (KIA) model (typically used for donation-based crowdfunding) the campaign promoter can keep the entire capital raised by the end of the campaign regardless of whether the funding goal has been reached or not (Cumming *et al.*, 2020).

Companies that intend to engage in equity crowdfunding financing usually have to present a pitch deck that summarises the business proposition, the history of the company and the main results, the business plan, the composition of the team, and other information of an economic-financial nature. The presentation of the pitch deck is then followed by an evaluation period of three to four weeks during which the platform conducts due diligence on the company and verifies the accuracy of the information provided. Unlike reward-based crowdfunding, the screening and pre-selection activity of equity crowdfunding platforms follows a structured process aimed at best matching the financing needs of candidate companies to the interests of potential investors. Therefore, in the case of equity crowdfunding, the platforms select the companies, and not vice versa, with very high rejection rates of the proposals presented. Once selected, the company negotiates the terms and conditions of the financing with the platform. From this moment on, the platform takes on a central role, using its wealth of information to support companies during the campaign and help them reduce information asymmetries (Löher, 2019).

2.3   Platforms' design

Equity crowdfunding platforms may adopt different shareholder structures, i.e., nominee and direct shareholder structures (Walthoff-Borm *et al.*, 2018). Some platforms like Crowdcube offer businesses the opportunity to choose between the nominee and the direct shareholding structure, while other platforms use a specific shareholding structure for all campaigns. The Seedrs platform, for example, exclusively adopts the nominee shareholder structure.

2.3.1   *Direct shareholder structure*

Direct shareholder structures allow crowd investors to become direct shareholders of the financed companies. In this case, each individual investor becomes a legally registered shareholder of the company, acquiring, holding, and managing the shares on their own behalf. Walthoff-Borm *et al.* (2018) find evidence that the direct shareholder structure increases the innovative performance of equity-crowdfunded companies in terms of stronger patent application activity related especially to international patents. The acquired shares may have voting and pre-emption rights (Signori and Vismara, 2018).

2.3.2   *Nominee structure*

In nominee structures, the equity-crowdfunded company appoints a nominee entity (which is usually the equity crowdfunding platform) to hold the shares on behalf of the beneficial owners (i.e., the crowd investors). In this way, the platform becomes the only legally registered shareholder of the company that acquires, holds, and manages each minority shareholder's shares. The nominee represents the interests of the beneficial holders (i.e., the former minor shareholders), taking votes and issuing consent on their behalf. The beneficiaries (i.e., the crowd investors) maintain the right to any benefits associated with the investment, such as tax relief and any future returns.

The nominee structure has numerous benefits, including tax management, regulatory compliance, and simplified corporate governance and company administration. Previous studies (e.g., (Walthoff-Borm *et al.*, 2018)) have shown that equity-crowdfunded companies financed through a nominee structure show higher financial performance and suffer lower losses in the two years following the campaign than those financed through a direct shareholder structure.

2.4   The regulatory context

Since its inception, equity crowdfunding has attracted the attention of national authorities and policymakers in all European countries as an important alternative source of finance for entrepreneurial ventures, especially SMEs and start-ups. Individual member states have defined their internal regulations and transposed the relevant European directives through national implementation laws, leading to a fragmented crowdfunding regulation with no real consistent, unequivocal legislation at the European level (Cicchiello, 2019). The following subparagraphs describe the equity crowdfunding regulation in force in the selected countries, namely, Italy, France, Spain, and the United Kingdom, as well as the regulatory harmonisation process implemented by the European Union (EU).

2.4.1 Italy

Italy was the first country in Europe to adopt a specific regulation on equity crowdfunding through the Decree-Law 179/2012 also known as 'Decreto Crescita 2.0' (Growth Decree 2.0) containing 'Further urgent measures for the growth of the country' and converted into Law 221 on 18 December 2012. The aim was to offer start-ups an alternative funding channel to counter the decline in bank lending due to the 2008–2009 financial crisis. The decree amended the existing rules of the Consolidated Law on Financial Intermediation (TUF – Testo Unico della Finanza) by introducing a definition of equity crowdfunding platform and establishing special provisions for its management (Sections 50-quinquies 'Management of portals for raising capital for innovative start-ups' and 100-ter 'Offers through portals for raising capital'). The decree also delegated the regulation of certain statutory aspects, such as investor relations and rules of conduct, to the National Commission for the Societies and the Stock Exchange (CONSOB – Commissione Nazionale per le Società e la Borsa), the public authority responsible for regulating the Italian financial markets. After an extensive public consultation, on 26 June 2013, CONSOB issued Regulation No. 18592 containing provisions on the collection of risk capital by innovative start-ups through online portals. At first, the public offer of financial instruments via authorised crowdfunding platforms was reserved only for 'Innovative start-ups', including start-ups with a social vocation, as defined by Article 25 of the Decree-Law 179/2012. Given the importance of equity crowdfunding as an alternative source of funding, over time its use was extended to:

• small and medium-sized enterprises (SMEs), as defined in Article 2, paragraph 1, letter f, of Regulation (EU) 2017/1129 of 14 June 2017, organised as a company under the law of a member state of the European Union or a party to the agreements on the European Economic Area;

- innovative start-ups, including those with a social vocation, as defined in Article 25, paragraphs 2 and 4, of the Decree-Law 179/2012, and tourism start-ups, as defined in Article 11-bis of Decree-Law 83 of 31 May 2014;
- innovative small and medium-sized enterprises (innovative SMEs), as defined by Article 4, paragraph 1, of Decree-Law 3 of 24 January 2015, containing 'Urgent measures for the banking and investment system' and converted with amendments by Law 33 of 24 March 2015;
- collective investment undertakings (CIUs) that invest predominantly in innovative start-ups and innovative SMEs;
- capital companies that invest primarily in innovative start-ups and innovative SMEs.

The long process of regulatory development ended with the entry into force, on 8 April 2023, of Legislative Decree no. 30, of 10 March 2023, implementing the European Regulation 2020/1503 relating to crowd-funding service providers for businesses, and amending Regulation (EU) 2017/1129 and Directive (EU) 2019/1937. The decree amends the Legislative Decree no. 58/1998 – the Consolidated Law on Financial Intermediation (TUF) – and introduces the definition of crowdfunding services as indicated in Article 2.1.a of the European Regulation. According to the provisions, crowdfunding services consist in *matching the business funding interests of investors and project owners through the use of a crowdfunding platform.* They include the facilitation of granting of loans, the placing without a firm commitment of transferable securities and admitted instruments for crowdfunding purposes issued by project owners or a special purpose vehicle, and the reception and transmission of client orders in relation to those transferable securities and admitted instruments for crowdfunding purposes. The decree also defines the competent national supervisory authorities pursuant to the European regulation and their respective activities. The Italian Securities and Exchange Commission (Consob) is entrusted with the task of authorising (and revoking), after consultation with the Bank of Italy, the licenses of crowdfunding service providers. As before, Consob remains the competent authority to ensure compliance with the obliga-tions imposed by the regulation on transparency and correctness and to identify the national provisions applicable to marketing communications disseminated throughout Italy, as well as to monitor the operations of crowdfunding portals. The Bank of Italy, on the other hand, is designated as the competent authority to ensure compliance with the obligations imposed by the regulation on capital adequacy, risk containment, and shareholdings that can be held, disclosure to be made to the public on the same matters. The Bank of Italy, by consulting Consob, can authorise (and revoke) the license as provider of crowdfunding services to banks, payment institutions, electronic money institutions, and financial intermediaries enroled in the register.

Further changes compared to the previous Italian regulation include:

- prohibition for platforms to place shares of collective investment undertakings (CIUs);
- possibility of raising risk capital also for companies other than innovative start-ups and innovative and traditional SMEs;
- possibility of placing minibonds also with retail investors;
- possibility of carrying out campaigns concerning indirect investments made through vehicle corporations only in certain cases;
- maximum funding limit for each company of €5 million over a year instead of €8 million;
- introduction for both equity and lending crowdfunding of an assessment of 'enhanced appropriateness' for non-sophisticated investors with a maximum investment limit.

2.4.2 France

In France, a first step to regulate crowdfunding was taken in 2014 through the entry into force of the Ordinance 2014–559 of 30 May 2014. The legal framework was later revised by Law no. 2015–990 of 6 August 2015, also known as the 'Macron Law', which introduced two specific statutes for crowdfunding platforms:

- Intermediaries in participatory financing (Intermediaire en Financement Participatif – IFP), for lending-based crowdfunding platforms, and since December 2016 also for donation and reward-based platforms;
- Participatory investment advisor (Conseiller en Investissement Participatif – CIP), for equity-based crowdfunding platforms.

The law established that both IFP and CIP platforms had to be authorised and operate under the supervision of the Authority for the Financial Markets (Autorité des Marchés Financiers – AMF) and the French Prudential Supervision and Resolution Authority (Autorité de Contrôle Prudentiel et de Résolution – ACPR). Equity-based platforms were given the option to adopt the status of investment service provider (Prestataire de Services d'Investissement – PSI) and offer a variety of additional investment services defined by the AMF. To qualify and operate with IFP or CIP status, platforms had to be enroled in the Single Register of Insurance, Banking, and Finance Intermediaries (*Registre Unique des Intermediaires en Assurance*) kept by the French association ORIAS. Platforms operating with the PSI status had to be enrolled in the Register of Financial Agents (Regafi).

The French crowdfunding regime has been extensively modified by Order 2021-1735 of 22 December 2021 and the subsequent Decree 2022–110 of 1 February 2022 which have adapted the national legislation to the new harmonised European regime (Regulation (EU) 2020/1503 on European crowdfunding service providers for business).

The new European crowdfunding regime abolishes the CIP and PSI status and introduces the new status of 'crowdfunding service provider' (*Prestataire de Services de Financement Participatif* – PSFP) for platforms offering crowdfunding in the form of financial securities (shares and bonds) and for so-called 'onerous' credits (loans with interest or without interest but with financial advantages).

Platforms with this status can offer crowdfunding investments throughout the EU as long as the crowdfunding offer is related to commercial activities and does not exceed, over a 12-month period, €5 million per project. The list of authorised PSFPs is available on the European Securities and Markets Authority (ESMA) website. The new regime also designates the AMF as the competent authority responsible for approving and withdrawing the PSFP license, as well as monitoring and sanctioning the activities of PSFP-licensed platforms. In the case of lending-based crowdfunding platforms, the AMF will operate in consultation with the ACPR. The European regulation does not cover crowdfunding platforms that offer funding in the form of donations, rewards, and free loans, as well as funding in the form of loans or securities for non-commercial projects. As a consequence, these platforms will continue to operate under IFP status.

2.4.3 *Spain*

Spain was the second country in Europe to adopt an ad-hoc regulation on equity and lending crowdfunding through Law 5/2015, of 27 April 2015, on the promotion of business financing also known as 'LFFE', Ley de Fomento de la Financiación Empresarial. Pursuant to Title V of the LEFE, containing the 'Legal regime of Participatory Financing Platforms (PFP)', crowdfunding platforms are defined as (Article 46): 'authorised companies whose activity consists in putting in contact, professionally and through the web, a plurality of natural or legal persons that offer financing in exchange for a monetary return (i.e., investors), with natural or legal persons who request financing in their own name to allocate them to a participatory financing project (i.e., promoters)'.

The aforementioned article does not apply when the financing obtained by the promoters takes place exclusively through donations, the sale of goods and services, or interest-free loans.

The content of Title V of the LEFE was repealed by Articles 14 and 15 of Law 18/2022, of 28 September 2022 on the creation and growth of businesses. The new Title V, which entered into force on 10 November 2022, has adapted the Spanish legislation to the legal regime established at the European level by Regulation (EU) 2020/1503, so that platforms authorised in Spain can freely provide their services throughout the territory of the EU. One of the main innovations introduced by European legislation compared to the pre-existing national legislation is the inclusion of a new 'portfolio management' category that allows crowdfunding platform managers to invest funds on behalf of investors. The new law also establishes a single individual investment limit per project for non-sophisticated investors, which is set as the greater of €1,000 or 5% of the investor's net worth (excluding real estate and pension funds).[1] Non-sophisticated investors will be able to invest beyond the limit; however, in this case, they will receive a risk warning, give their explicit consent to the crowdfunding service provider, and demonstrate that they understand the investment and its risks. Furthermore, the law sets an investment limit of 5 million euros per project, which can be exceeded up to the limit established by the legislation of each member state, beyond which the issue of a prospectus is required (in this case it will not be possible to benefit from the European passport and the project will be submitted for fundraising only within that member state). The European Union Regulation does not apply to those platforms that only mediate participatory financing offers for an amount greater than €5,000,000, despite the fact that these types of platforms were included in the scope of application of Law 5/2015, of April 27. It is for this reason that Article 14 regulates the figure of 'non-harmonised platforms', so that these platforms are not in a situation of lack of legal certainty and clarity.

In addition to adapting to European legislation, the amendment to Title V allows crowdfunding platforms to create and group investors: (i) in a limited liability company, whose corporate object and sole activity consists in holding shares in the company in which they participate; (ii) in an institution regulated by the National Securities Market Commission; or (iii) in other figures commonly used for such purposes in other member states of the EU. Although the legislation previously in force in Spain did not prohibit this possibility, it did not actually occur. The legislator has therefore deemed it convenient to expressly include it in the legislation, assimilating the Spanish legal system to that of other neighbouring countries and promoting a measure that can have positive effects on the growth and functioning of crowdfunding platforms.

2.4.4 The United Kingdom

In the United Kingdom, the Financial Conduct Authority (FCA) has regulated regulation equity-based and lending-based crowdfunding since

2014 with the entry into force of Policy Statement PS14/4. Unlike lending-based crowdfunding, which constitutes a standalone regulated activity, equity-based crowdfunding falls within the existing activities under the Regulated Activities Order (RAO), which includes 'arranging deals in investments' and 'making arrangements with a view to transactions in investments'. Existing requirements relating to the offering of private shares to the public under the Companies Act 2006 and the United Kingdom listing and prospectus regime also apply to equity-based crowdfunding. In addition to FCA regulation, the UK Crowdfunding Association (UKCFA), a self-regulatory trade body set up in 2013, has established a code of conduct focused primarily on investor protection that its members must comply with. Since equity-based crowdfunding is considered by the FCA as 'a high-risk investment activity' due to the potential partial or total loss of the invested capital, these platforms are prohibited from marketing illiquid speculative securities (SISs), such as mini-bonds, to retail investors. Following the United Kingdom's exit from the EU in 2020 (also known as Brexit), the EU Regulation 2020/1503 on 'European crowdfunding service providers for business' does not apply to UK-based crowdfunding platforms. These platforms will continue to operate under the current UK regulation and will need to be authorised if they want to operate in any of the EU member states.

2.4.5   *The regulatory harmonisation process*

Given the growing importance of crowdfunding (particularly in the equity-based form) in supporting entrepreneurial projects normally excluded from traditional financing channels (Estrin *et al.*, 2018), individual member states have adopted internal regulations over time shaped according to the characteristics and needs of local markets and investors (Cicchiello *et al.*, 2020). As shown in the previous paragraphs, some countries have enacted ad hoc regulatory frameworks, while others have adapted the scope of existing regulatory frameworks to the opportunities and risks posed by crowdfunding (Gabison, 2014). In both cases, the aim of the various policymakers at the national level was to encourage the growth of crowdfunding while ensuring the stability of the internal market and an adequate level of transparency and investor protection. However, the fragmented nature and differences in regulation of crowdfunding between individual member states have led to increased transaction costs and prevented crowdfunding platforms from expanding their cross-border activities in the EU (European Commission, 2017b). Furthermore, the variety of national regulations in terms of securities regulation and investor protection has led to a state of uncertainty which for a long time has represented a major obstacle to the development of this alternative financing tool. According to Ziegler *et al.* (2019), the European crowdfunding market remained underdeveloped compared to the rest of the world mainly due to the lack of regulatory coherence between different member states.

In order to answer the above-mentioned regulatory challenges, the EU has started a process of harmonisation of crowdfunding regulation in Europe aimed at removing regulatory diversity, establishing a level playing field for all involved actors, and ensuring a high level of investor protection (Cicchiello, 2020). Over the years there have been numerous interventions by the European Commission (see Cicchiello and Leone, 2020) starting with the *Action Plan on Building a Capital Markets Union* (COM (2015) 468 final) published on 30 September 2015. Issued, among other things, with the aim of increasing the role of alternative finance (including crowdfunding) in the EU member states, the Action Plan highlighted the lack of a single legal framework for crowdfunding and the need to develop a European regulation that would balance the objectives of investor protection with those of crowdfunding expansion (European Commission, 2015). The Action Plan was followed by the Commission staff working document on *Crowdfunding in the EU Capital Markets Union* (SWD (2016) 154 final) published in May 2016 (European Commission, 2016) and the report *Accelerating the Capital Markets Union: Addressing National Barriers to Capital Flows* (COM (2017) 147 final) published in March 2017 (European Commission, 2017a).

The European Commission confirmed its intention to implement a common European regulatory framework for crowdfunding through the publication in March 2018 of the *FinTech Action Plan: For a more competitive and innovative European financial sector* (COM (2018) 109 final) (European Commission, 2018a). The FinTech Plan included the *proposal for an EU Regulation on investment-based and lending-based crowdfunding service providers (ECSP) for business* (COM (2018) 113 final) (European Commission, 2018b). On 7 October 2020, the European Union approved Regulation (EU) 2020/1503 of the European Parliament and of the Council on *European crowdfunding service providers for business, and amending Regulation (EU) 2017/1129 and Directive (EU) 2019/1937* (European Union, 2020). This EU Regulation establishes a complete and exhaustive legal regime for crowdfunding platforms. Its purpose is to unify the regulation at the European level, so that crowdfunding platforms authorised and supervised in accordance with the EU Regulation can freely provide their services throughout the territory of the EU, without the need to obtain a different authorisation in each member state in which they want to provide their services.

The European Regulation introduces the following changes:

• the creation of a single register of all crowdfunding service providers at the European Securities and Markets Authority (ESMA);

- the obligation to provide investors with a standardised information document (Key Investment Information Sheet, KIIS) reflecting the specific features and risks of lending-based and investment-based crowdfunding;
- the introduction of more stringent rules on conflict of interest and incentives for platforms, which include, for example, a ban on managers from accepting offers published on their platform;
- the provision of prudential requirements in terms of minimum capital and business continuity.

Since the approval of Regulation (EU) 2020/1503, national regulatory regimes on equity crowdfunding have largely been replaced by the European legal regime. The UK government has confirmed that the European Regulation will not be transposed into the national regime established in 2013.

2.5   Tax relief

In response to the growing importance of equity-based crowdfunding as an alternative funding channel for early-stage unlisted companies, European policymakers started offering tax incentive schemes to encourage investors and help them mitigate some of the risks involved in crowdfunding investment (Cicchiello *et al.*, 2019). By offering investors the opportunity to purchase shares into early-stage companies while providing a range of generous tax reliefs, the tax incentive schemes have become increasingly attractive to the European equity crowdfunding space over the past two and a half decades. The following subparagraphs describe the tax incentive schemes for equity-based crowdfunding in force in France, Spain, the United Kingdom, Belgium, and Italy (the only countries that adopt tax incentives to encourage equity-based crowdfunding). Table 2.1 shows the tax incentive schemes in force in the analysed countries.

2.5.1   *France*

To encourage taxpayers to invest their savings in SMEs, French regulators have developed various tax incentive systems for investments made also, but not only, through equity crowdfunding platforms. The Madelin or IR-PME tax reduction (Réduction d'impôt Madelin) allows natural persons to reduce the amount of their income tax (impôt sur le revenu – IR) by 25% (18% before 10 August 2020) of the sums invested, directly or through a holding company or investment funds, in the previous year in the capital of unlisted French and European SMEs. To benefit from the tax reduction, investors must hold the shares for at least five years and the investment must have taken place before December 31 of the fiscal year.

Table 2.1 Overview of the tax incentive schemes in force in the analysed countries

Country	Incentive scheme	Benefits
France	Tax reduction Madelin (IR-PME)	Natural persons are entitled to reduce the amount of their income tax by 25% of the sums invested, directly or through a holding company or investment funds, in the previous year in the capital of unlisted French and European SMEs.
	Equity Saving Plan (PEA)	Investors are entitled to a tax exemption for capital gains, dividends, and other income related to their investments in securities issued by French and European companies up to €150,000 per year.
	Equity Saving Plan for SMEs (PEA-PME-ETI)	Investors are entitled to a tax exemption for capital gains, dividends, and other income related to their investments in securities issued by French and European SMEs and Mid Cap companies up to €75,000 per year.
Spain	Tax deduction	Investors in newly or recently established company are entitled to a 30% deduction in their income tax up to a maximum of €60,000 of the total investment.
United Kingdom	Enterprise Investment Scheme (EIS)	Investors are entitled to: • Tax relief of 30% on investments of up to £1 million per tax year (or up to £2 million for investment in knowledge-intensive companies); • Tax-free capital gains if the shares are held for a minimum of 3 years; • Capital gains tax deferral up to 50% of the tax liability; • Loss relief against both income tax and capital gains tax. Companies are entitled to: raise up to £5 million each year, with a maximum of £12 million in their lifetime.
	Seed Enterprise Investment Scheme (SEIS)	Investors are entitled to: • Tax relief of 50% on investments of up to £200,00 per tax year; • Tax-free capital gains if the shares are held for a minimum of 3 years; • Capital gains tax relief up to a maximum of £50,000 on gains that are reinvested in EIS-eligible shares in the same tax year; • Loss relief against any of the investor's taxable earnings.

(Continued)

Table 2.1 (Continued)

Country	Incentive scheme	Benefits
Belgium	Tax Shelter for investment in Belgian start-ups, scale-ups, SMEs, and microenterprises	Companies are entitled to: raise up to £150,000 per year. Investors are entitled to deduct from their personal income tax or non-resident tax: • 25% of the amount invested in scale-ups; • 30% of the amount invested in SMEs; and • 45% of the amount invested in start-ups. • Scale-ups are entitled to raise up to €1,000,000 per year. • SMEs (or start-ups) are entitled to raise up to €500,000 per year. • Micro-enterprises (or early-stage start-ups) are entitled to raise up to €500,000 per year.
Italy	Tax incentives for investments in innovative start-ups and SMEs	Natural persons are entitled to deduct from their personal income tax 30% of the amount invested in innovative start-ups and SMEs up to €1,000,000 per year. Legal entities are entitled to deduct from their corporate income tax 30% of the amount invested in innovative start-ups and SMEs up to €1,800,000 per year.

Source: Author's elaboration.

The tax benefit is limited to €50,000 for single, widowed, and divorced people and €100,000 for married couples or couples who are signatories of the Civil Solidarity Pact (Pacs), subject to joint taxation. Investors can carry forward the tax reduction for the fraction of investments exceeding the annual limit for the following four years (right to carry forward).

Equity savings plans (Plan d'Epargne en Actions – PEA), as well as equity savings plans intended for the financing of SMEs and Mid Cap companies (Plan d'Épargne en Actions dédié aux Petites et Moyennes Entreprises – PEA-PME-ETI), allow French individuals to benefit from a tax exemption for capital gains, dividends, and other income related to their investments in equity issued by companies located in the EU member states and certain member states of the European Economic Area (EEA). To benefit from the tax exemption, investors must hold the shares for at least five years. The traditional equity savings plan (PEA) allows investments in securities issued by companies without capitalisation constraints up to €150,000 per taxpayer per year. The PEA-PME-ETI regime allows investments in securities issued by SMEs and Mid Cap companies (ETI) that meet the following requirements: (i) have fewer than 5,000 employees and (ii) an annual turnover below €1,500,000 or a total balance sheet below €2,000,000. Investors (in the case of direct purchase) or investment funds must evaluate the presence of these criteria when acquiring the securities.

The maximum investable amount in this savings plan is €75,000 per taxpayer per year. Investments eligible for both PEA and PEA-PMI-ETI may be made directly or indirectly through investment funds, French funds, and foreign funds authorised for distribution in France, as long as such entities invest at least 75% of their assets in eligible assets.

The Madelin or IR-PME tax reduction cannot be combined with that of the Equity Savings Plan (PEA or PEA-PME).

2.5.2 Spain

In Spain, natural persons who invest in newly or recently created company (no more than three years) through equity crowdfunding platforms are entitled to a 30% deduction in their income tax (IRPF – Impuesta sobre la renta de las personas fisicas) up to a maximum of €60,000 of the total investment. The tax deduction does not apply to investors acting as legal entities and is subject to the following requirements:

• The newly or recently established company must have one of the following legal status: public limited company (PLC), limited liability company (LLC), employee-owned companies (sociedad anónima laboral), or employment-owned limited liability company (sociedad de responsabilidad limitada laboral).

- The newly or recently established company cannot exercise the management of movable or real estate assets as a business activity, and it must carry out an activity for which it has sufficient personal and material resources.
- The equity capital of the newly or recently established company cannot exceed €400,000 at the beginning of the tax period. Also, the company must be newly established or no older than three years.
- The investor cannot hold more than 40% of the share capital of the newly or recently established company in which he has invested. In addition, the investor must hold the capital for a minimum of three years and a maximum of twelve years and must obtain a certificate of participation in the capital certifying the possession of all the aforementioned requirements.

2.5.3   *The United Kingdom*

The United Kingdom offers attractive tax relief schemes for all crowdfunding models, with the exception of reward-based crowd-funding, the application of which is provided and monitored by Her Majesty's Revenue and Customs (HMRC). These schemes aim to stimulate the use of crowdfunding among UK companies and investors. The Gift Aid scheme is a government scheme that allows UK taxpayers to claim back 25p of tax for every £1 they donate to qualified charities through, but not limited to, donation-based crowdfunding platforms. As will be described in Chapter 3, peer-to-peer (P2P) lending crowdfunding offers lenders (who are UK tax residents) tax relief consisting of a 12-month carry-back through the Innovative Finance ISA Scheme (IFISA). The Enterprise Investment Scheme (EIS) and the Seed Enterprise Investment Scheme (SEIS) are available for projects taking place on equity-based crowdfunding platforms. The EIS and the SEIS, together with the Social Investment Tax Relief (SITR) and the Venture Capital Trust (VCT), represent the four venture capital schemes designed to help SMEs and social enterprises in the United Kingdom attract the investment they need to grow. All these schemes offer tax reliefs to individuals who buy and hold new shares, bonds, or assets for a specific period of time.

The Enterprise Investment Scheme (EIS) was launched in 1994 to help small unlisted companies raise capital by giving their investors tax relief as an incentive to purchase those companies' shares. This scheme allows companies – within seven years of their first commercial sale – to raise up to £5 million each year, with a maximum of £12 million in a company's lifetime (including the amounts received from other venture capital schemes by any subsidiaries, former subsidiaries, or businesses acquired).

look, making them feel good about themselves and helping them become whatever they want to become.

In 2004, Dove launched a groundbreaking advertising campaign, called Real Beauty, which showcased women of all shapes, colors, and sizes being held up as real standards of beauty. This was one of the first cases of a brand stating what its purpose was. Dove was not just selling soap and other beauty products: it was empowering women – long before the #metoo movement. Dove kept going at it, highlighting this subject again and again and again, year after year after year, for almost two decades now. This brand stand became a staple for brands in the 21st century.

Dove wasn't the first, though. Before Dove, there was a revolutionary television commercial by Nike, from 1995, called "If you let me play". It showed several girls speaking to the camera and telling their parents and the audience all the wonderful things that would happen in their lives if "you let me play sports". Things like "I'll be more likely to leave a husband who beats me" and "I will like myself more". But it was one shot. A relevant, inspiring beautifully produced piece of brand communication, no doubt, but a drop of water in an ocean of Nike sports messages.

Before Dove and Nike, however, there was a pioneer fashion brand which was the talk of the town for its daring brand efforts. Benetton's 1980s and 1990s famous advertising campaigns, created by Oliviero Toscani under the "united colors of Benetton" tagline, were the first to systematically showcase sensitive social themes such as racism, HIV, religion, war, the death sentence, or the destruction of natural habitats. Benetton used its advertising paid media, such as billboards and print adverts, to raise awareness for several social problems. However, contrary to current brand trends, the brand did not choose a specific purpose. Even though the "united colors" tended to highlight anti-racism, the brand kept its multi-purpose positioning.

This is the legacy brands have to live up to. As previously stated, having great products that outperform the competition is not enough. Being cool and innovative is not enough. Being used by "beautiful people" is not enough. Modern brands have to be driven by purpose in order to become accepted as viable options for modern stakeholders.

One of the pioneers of brand purpose was Simon Sinek, who introduced the idea in a 2009 Ted Talk intitled "How Great Leaders Inspire Action". Sinek famously said "people don't buy what you do; they buy why you do it. The goal is not to do business with everybody who needs what you have. The goal is to do business with people who believe what you believe". Brands got the message.

4.3.4 Physicality

In a virtual infinite digital world, physicality is expected to become a life-gourmet experience. It will become scarce and rare, by comparison. Brands which deal with material products can expect to be paid premium price, premium attention, and premium engagement. Digital products are easily replicated, thus becoming less valuable.

Still, physical products and services will be flawed by risk. Human interaction has dangers and perils most people will want to skip. In the digital world there's no perception of immediate risk or body harm. It's a controlled environment. People may be bullied, their accounts hacked, and their intimate photos shared, but even if it can be pride threatening, it's never life threatening. People can unplug anytime. They are in control.

4.3.5 *Leveraging equities with unlikely partners, platforms, and themes*

In a post-pandemic highly volatile world, brands most adopt an adaptation-mode posture at all times. They should thus prepare for change continuously, challenging themselves to stretch its brand arms and move into uncharted waters, such as creating partnerships with unlikely brands or crossing-over to unlikely subjects, and see what happens.

Quite naturally fashion brands are pioneering this trend, putting themselves to the test, and watching how their brand communities react.

Luxury fashion brand Balenciaga well-known for its collaboration with celeb Kim Kardashian created a ten-minute online episode for long-running TV series The Simpsons, featuring Homer Simpson posing as a top-model in a Balenciaga outfit. It also ventured into the gaming market developing a tie-in with Fortnite online video game, creating skins (digital clothes) which players can buy for its characters. Burberry did the same by launching a collection of NFT (non-fungible token, a unique digital object which can't be replaced) for Blankos Block Party, an open-world multiplayer online game.

In 2022 Balenciaga launched a theme-sensitive campaign for kids clothing which showed children holding BDSM-themed teddy bears. The online community's reaction was swift and brutal. Children remain an understandable highly sensitive topic. Calls for cancelling brand came from everywhere. All Balenciaga partners, including Kim Kardashian, pondered terminating the brand-partnership. The brand quickly issued a public apology. In this interconnected world, brand scrutiny from all stakeholders is the norm and should be embraced.

Also, modern brands have to be able to adapt to new platforms. Besides gaming, brands should add voice (Alexa, Siri, Google assistant, and more), podcasts (audio content which had a huge boost during the pandemic lockdowns), or the multiverse.

The path for contemporary brands will always be on the crossroad of order and chaos. Brands have to be authentic, true to themselves. But they also have to cross new boundaries into the unknown, experimenting new ways of interacting with new themes and partners which will put its authenticity to the test, and arise tension between what the brand is and what the brand will be.

4.3.6 Complexify to simplify

The simplicity of images, values, messages, stories, that brands covet, so they can become attractive for new audiences, will require an intricate balance of multiple factors, from products and point-of-sales to platforms and people.

Just as organisms became increasingly complex throughout 3 billion years of natural evolution, brand systems are becoming increasingly complex in the new digital world, as they find new ways to remain coherent while working with multiple platforms, multiple devices, multiple stakeholders, multiple communities, multiple languages, multiple themes, multiple messages, multiple events, and multiple *whatever*.

Not only thinking and planning but also creating and producing will become of the essence.

4.3.7 Digital mutations

Digitality is not just a tool, a technology, or even a landscape. As previously explained in this chapter, it is an alternative reality which is transforming human nature and by extension, brand nature – as people and brands follow an infinite feedback loop.

It's evolving, encompassing generative AI, the multiverse, and in the process being changed by them.

Generative AI tools will have a direct impact on brand creation. Looking at the answers AI tools provide one can't help but feel that an "umbilical cord" has been clamped and cut somewhere.

When prompted the question "how do you explain the importance generative AI can have for brands?", ChatGPT, a free tool created by OpenAI company, provides a mind-blowing answer as thorough as we would expect from a sales person:

> *Generative AI can have a number of important implications for brands, as it can help them create new and unique content, improve their customer engagement, and even automate many of their tedious tasks. Here are a few specific examples of how generative AI could be used by brands:*
>
> * *Content creation: Generative AI can be used to automatically generate new and unique images, videos, and other forms of content. This can help brands quickly create large amounts of content without having to rely on human labor. Additionally, generative AI can be used to personalize content based on a customer's preferences and behavior, which could help increase engagement and sales.*

- *Product design: Generative AI can be used to quickly generate new product designs that can be tested and iterated on, rather than doing so manually. This can help companies develop products faster, and in a more cost-effective way.*
- *Personalization: Generative AI can be used to analyze customer data and generate personalized product recommendations, customized emails and messages to each customer, which can help increase customer loyalty and retention.*
- *Advertising: Generative AI can be used to automatically generate new and unique ad campaigns and to optimize them based on performance. This can help companies reach their target audience more effectively and can help improve the ROI on their advertising spend.*
- *Customer service: Generative AI can be used to automatically generate responses to customer inquiries, and chatbot can be used to interact with customers in a more natural way. This can help companies provide better and more efficient customer service, and can also help to automate repetitive and mundane tasks.*

Overall, generative AI can help brands create new and unique content, improve their customer engagement, and automate their tedious tasks. By using these AI-based tools, companies can gain a competitive edge in the market, and can also improve their bottom line.

As the creation of brands mutates with AI tools, it is easy to forget that brands need to interact with human stakeholders to become... brands. In the digital AI realm, the creation of brands who only interact with AI agents will not be necessary – for the near future.

The multiverse will provide a different brand experience for consumers, changing the way people perceive and interact with brands, empowering brand communities, for instance.

As Wayne Deakin, Global Principal Creative at brand agency Wolff Olins, frames it,

In today's multichannel, multi-device world, the stuff of science fiction is fast-becoming fact. The boundary between real and virtual worlds is a blur. Parallel universes exist, along with multiple versions of our own identities. And we can be somewhere and then everywhere in a single click or swipe.
(Creative Review, Feb/Mar 2022, p.22)

This new multiverse reality is so different from the natural world that new brand principles emerge, according to Deacon.

The first is *acceptance*. Brands have to accept their limitations. Not all brands will save the world, be cool, or entertain. Brands will have to know their place. Some will be center stage, such as Adidas, Apple, and countless others; some will be ingredient brands, a sort of molecules for *center stage brands*, such as Intel, and countless business-to-business brands. Both brand types can be relevant and authentic.

The second principle is *flexibility*. Deakin says, "one brand may be experienced most as a conversational interface – say, via Alexa. Another might be primarily experienced in a shop. Both, however, will also need to find the tools and tactics to be (…) anywhere" (Creative Review, Feb/Mar 2022, p.24). As mentioned before, brands will have to be able to adapt to new channels, new devices, and new communities.

The third principle is *coherence*. Wayne Deakin again, "it's about saying fundamentally the same thing but in different ways for different spaces".

Acceptance, flexibility, and coherence are principles brand creators will likely follow when designing the new multilayered multiverse multi-landscapes, but as digitalization grows for society and all its communities it follows that these guidelines will be applied to all social brands in their never-ending quest to reach new ways of engaging and establishing a relationship with people.

References

Creative Review. (February/March 2022). *The Future Issue, 42*(1), 22–25.

Lipovetsky, G. (2021). *Le sacré de l'authenticité*. Paris: Gallimard.

Merz, M. A., He, Y., & Vargo, S. L. (2009). The evolving brand logic: A service-dominant logic perspective. *Journal of the Academy of Marketing Science, 37*(3), 328–344.

Morhart, F., Malär, L., Guèvremont, A., Girardin, F., & Grohmann, B. (2015). Brand authenticity: An integrative framework and measurement scale. *Journal of Consumer Psychology, 25*(2), 200–218.

Negroponte, N. (1995). *Being digital*, 1st edition. New York: Alfred A. Knopf.

Olins, W. (2014). *Brand new, the shape of brands to come*. London: Thames & Hudson.

Schwartz, B. (2004). *The paradox of choice*. New York: Harper Perennial.

5 How to become a social brand

Patrícia Dias

CECC/ Universidade Católica Portuguesa

This chapter begins with a discussion about how the digital environment and brands shape each other and about the challenges and opportunities that brands face in contemporary times.

Then, this chapter presents a discussion of the features, strategies, and tactics that can make a brand stand out from its competitors and matter to its consumers and fans.

Finally, this chapter draws on previous findings and literature on the topic to suggest a new model that can help brands cope successfully with the contemporary digital environment. To stand out and matter, brands must become Social Brands.

5.1 How brands can stand out and matter in the contemporary digital environment

Contemporary society is, and has been for the past few decades, profoundly shaped by the dissemination and evolution of digital technologies. These have a strong impact on social structures and individual agency (Giddens, 1986), so much so that the Mediatization Theory has suggested that they have become a meta-structure within which all the others, as well as individual agents, are framed (Hepp et al., 2015).

This deep impact encompasses a contradiction between the promise that digital technologies would make tasks quicker and make our lives easier, when in fact the increase in information in circulation worldwide and in the amount of communication stimuli that we are targeted with every day causes an overwhelmness that results in a busier and more accelerated pace of life. Thus, we live in a world of abundance of similar offers and of scarcity of time and attention (and often budget) on the part of consumers (Davenport & Beck, 2001).

In the contemporary accelerated, dynamic, fluid, and ephemeral phygital context (Mamina & Tolstikova, 2020), brands not only face numerous challenges but can also benefit from many opportunities.

One of the main challenges is standing out from competitors in a global market filled with so many similar offers, and thus conquering the attention of

DOI: 10.4324/9781003382331-6

busy potential customers that lead accelerated lives. Brands can act as a beacon for consumers, as they provide familiarity and trust. In the face of many possibilities and scarcity of time to ponder on them all, customers often turn to brands that are familiar. Thus, building awareness is crucial for brands. The fact that contemporary consumers tend not to be very loyal adds to this challenge, as it is not only a matter of conquering the customers for the first time, but keeping them is equally as challenging, as they keep browsing for better offers. Another important challenge is that contemporary customers have more media literacy and trust more on the reviews and recommendations of other customers than they do on the promotional communication of brands. The digital environment provides an outlet with great potential reach for customers to share their experiences, positive or negative, which can therefore result in valuable word of mouth or in grave reputational crises. To reach consumers in a more influential way, brands must conquer other consumers and turn them into brand ambassadors that feed a renewed consumer journey, in which the post-purchase phase gains importance (van Bommel et al., 2014).

When we look at the opportunities, these appear as the reverse face of the coin that we were facing when considering the challenges. If getting attention, maintaining engagement, and generating loyalty have become more difficult, brands must focus on new strategies to work on these challenges. One opportunity arises from the fact that, from a psychological and sociological perspective, the way people form their identity, perceive their auto-representation, and express their self-presentation is changing. Before the digitalization of society, identity was intimately related to rigid structures that frame everyone, which are socially constructed and expressed through culture. Identity was built around the place of birth, and individuals felt intimately related to their own local community and their families. Currently, people travel more and have more international experiences such as studying abroad or emigrating, people consume news and entertainment from other countries and are familiar with diversity, people shop in a global market and feel like they are "citizens of the world". Another structuring feature of identity used to be religion. Our religious beliefs, through practice or merely because they are embedded in the culture that surrounds us, determine our values and our notion of right and wrong, and these guide our action. Currently, living in a global and diverse world, individuals have become more inquisitive and critical about religious beliefs, norms, and practices that are passed on as "tradition" and are more open to several paths to personal growth in their quest to be connected with a spiritual dimension. Finally, the structure of families, the notion of relationships, and the construction of gender itself have become more diversified and fluid (Castells, 1996).

Individuals may feel overwhelmed and a bit lost when facing this liquification of social structures (Bauman, 2000). They are looking for new ways to discover their identity, to express it, and to connect with others, and brands can provide the "vocabulary" they need (Kornberger, 2010). Consumers can appropriate brands to express themselves and to build their self-presentation, which can correspond to their self-representation or be a projection of how they desire to be or be perceived. Either way, consumers tend to appropriate brands they identify with, and this identification can reach different levels of depth. Consumers may pick a brand because it fits their lifestyle, it helps them enjoy the lifestyle they appreciate and gain social status through the recognition of others. Going a bit deeper, individuals may pick a brand if there is a correspondence between their personality and the personality of the brand. If a brand communicates its identity as being bold and a consumer self-perceives or wants to be perceived as bold, the brand may be appropriated to express that specific feature, thus building the desired self-presentation. Finally, if a brand expresses certain values and those values resonate with the consumers, they may pick that brand because it talks about or is active about an issue that is extremely important for them, and they may appropriate the brand as part of their own activism (Kotler et al., 2017).

Thus, connecting with consumers through shared values emerges as a successful way of coping with the challenging contemporary environment. Are the brands that communicate and act on values that resonate with their targets more successful? It that crucial to being a "good" brand in contemporary society?

5.2   What makes a brand "good"

At first, the field of marketing was born under the common assumption in the fields of economy and management that states that consumers are rational and will therefore opt for the offer that represents the best balance possible between quality and price. This assumption led the first marketing theories to focus on the optimization of production, which afforded a cut on costs and a widening of profit margins. As markets shifted from an excess of demand to an excess of supply, marketing shifted its focus to how to prevail over competitors that present similar offers. The focus was now on products and services, on differentiating the offer from competitors. Brands became more important, as they contributed to differentiating by adding intangible value to products and services. This resulted mainly from brand associations – with narratives, with personality traits, with inspiration, and with desires – all of which made products more attractive to consumers, therefore apporting added value both to consumers and to companies. As branding established itself as an important field in marketing, researchers turned their attention to the features that made a brand more successful than others.

Aaker (1996), researching about what he described as "strong" brands, came up with the concept of brand equity (Aaker, 1991), a model intended for measuring both the tangible and intangible dimensions of the value that a brand can add to products or services. The initial brand equity model had five dimensions: (1) brand awareness (the amount of consumers and potential consumers that know the brand, recognize the brand, and are able to recall the brand when facing certain needs); (2) perceived quality (the value that consumers and potential consumers recognize in the products or services of a certain brand, the maximum amount that they are willing to pay for them); (3) brand associations (the brand's ability to create an image in the consumers and potential consumers' minds that is associated to certain emotions, narratives, experiences, aspirations, and desires); and (4) brand loyalty (the extent to which a consumer remains loyal to the brand when presented with other options). Aaker (1996) also suggested a scale to measure brand equity.

This concept has been developed by several authors and remains central in branding. According to a literature review on the topic, de Chernatony and Christodoulides (2004) summarized the value that brands can afford both to companies and to consumers. To companies, brands enhance the efficiency of marketing efforts and maximize marketing investment; brands can generate competitive advantage by stressing differentiation from competitors; brands can expand profit margins because consumers are willing to pay more for a product or service of a certain brand; brands can increase and consolidate loyalty; and brands can also facilitate brand extension, helping companies venture in new markets based on high awareness, strong brand image, and positive reputation. To consumers, brands facilitate the consumer journey, particularly the initial stages of search and pondering; brands reiterate trust throughout the whole consumer journey; and, more importantly, brands can increase the satisfaction that a product or service affords to consumers because of the brand associations.

Pappu, Quester, and Cooksey (2005) have found strong correlations between all of these dimensions of brand equity, which means that when a brand is strong in some of these features, it reflects positively on others, but the reverse also happens.

More recently, an alternative concept has emerged in marketing to address the potential that a brand has to be successful. If brand equity stresses the value that a brand affords and attempts to measure it, this alternative way of thinking about what makes a brand "good" focuses on its ability to create and nurture a meaningful relationship with consumers and fans throughout time. This alternative view is based on the concept of brand love. Carroll and Ahuvia (2005) explain that the concept of brand love is inspired in psychology theories that explain how people develop strong attachments to objects, to the extent that it can be comparable to the affection that arises between to people, that is, to love. As is the case of love, the authors argue that brand love can be more or less passionate, more or less intense, temporary or lifelong. Even in these various shapes or forms, brand love consists of a strong emotional attachment to a brand that materializes in a consistent preference for such brand and in "declarations of love". It is not mandatory being a consumer for loving a brand. You can be only a fan and even so afford value to the brand through your active engagement with the brand and through your positive word of mouth. We make like many people, but we love only so many.

Each consumer has their own set of "love brands", and it is not easy to be a part of this exclusive circle. In their literature review on the topic, Carroll and Ahuvia (2006) have identified numerous antecedents of brand love, that is, features that brands can incorporate or develop and that significantly contribute for them to become love brands in the eyes of consumers. The authors have also explored the consequences of brand love, that is, what brands have to gain by investing in becoming love brands. Aaker (2020), more recently, also offered further insights into what features drive the success of a brand and which outcomes result from it.

Concerning antecedents, love brands afford hedonism. Products and services under such insignia are enjoyable and appeal to our senses. A pleasant aroma, a nice texture to touch, aesthetic symmetry and proportion, a relaxing sound, a provocative taste, all of these elements can contribute to an enjoyable experience of fruition that delights the consumer. These hedonistic features are usually associated with a high perception of quality that consumers and potential consumers associate with a love brand. In addition, love brands tend to be prestigious, as the recognition of such brands as "good" or valuable by others affords their consumers social status. Furthermore, consumers or fans relate to brands based on affinities between their self-representation and the identity that brands communicate. The identification between consumers or fans and brands may occur on different levels – lifestyle, identity or personality, and values – but it is a strong requirement for a brand to become a love brand. It is not possible to connect to a brand on such level if there isn't identification. Identification is intertwined with self-expression (or self-presentation). If a consumer or fan identifies with a brand, they can appropriate it to express their own identity, perceived or desired. When a brand is used for self-expression, it can be perceived as part of oneself. Finally, another important dimension that the authors have identified is that love brands afford consumers and fans a sense of belonging to a community of people who share the same preferences, interests, and values. This feature has become particularly important after the Covid-19 pandemic, during which many experienced tough lockdown periods with very limited social interaction. Forced to follow safety rules of social distancing when in person and facing the limitations of digital interactions, people struggled to staying connected, people craved human contact, and people revalued sociability. Brands that offer such connections, particularly with others that share not only our lifestyle or personality traits, but especially our values, have more potential for fostering brand love.

Of course, if all brands are trying to become love brands, and each consumer only loves a restricted set of brands, it is a fierce struggle in which brands invest a lot of resources. Why is it worth fighting to become a love brand? Being a love brand provides many advantages. Consumers are fiercely, and sometimes stubbornly, loyal to their love brands. They always prefer their love brands, and they might even refuse to consume others, even if their favorite is unavailable. Consumers are willing to make sacrifices for the brands they love. The most common sacrifice is paying more, but consumers will go to great lengths for their love brands, such as waiting if the brand is temporarily unavailable, trading down on other choices so that they can trade up on their love brand, traveling a long distance to find their love brand, etc. Another positive outcome of being a love brand is generating positive word of mouth from consumers and fans. When consumers and fans love a brand, they like to share such love with the world and therefore become brands ambassadors or evangelizers. The digital environment boosts such declarations of love, and each consumer or fan can reach a potentially wide audience. In addition, consumers and fans like to engage with their love brands, and they can add value by creating content on social media, by being active on brands communities, or simply by incorporating the brand in their daily lives.

Following on Aaker's footsteps (1996), Roberts (2005) developed a model to measure to each extent a brand is a lovemark. The author defines a lovemark as a brand that a consumer prefers and is loyal to, even if it is not necessary or not suitable for him – he gives as an example his own experience, one of his lovemarks is a hair shampoo, which he doesn't need because he is bald, but he enjoys the experience of washing his hair with the said shampoo, particularly the foam and the aroma. In his model, a lovemark stands on two pillars, love and respect. If you love a brand but you don't respect it, it is an ephemeral infatuation, a fad. If you respect a brand, but you don't love it, you may buy, but only until a better alternative presents itself. Roberts (2005) offers further detail on each of these two pillars. In order to evoke respect, a brand must offer a performance that matches its promotions and that corresponds to the expectations of consumers (preferable that exceeds them). In addition, its communication must be transparent and honest, so that trust is earned. Ultimately, trustworthiness results in a consolidated positive reputation. In order to arouse love, a brand must be sensual, which is similar to hedonism in the sense that a brand can appeal to all the five senses to propitiate the fruition of enjoyable experiences or, simply put, pleasure. Also, a brand must build an intimate space in which identification on the part of consumer towards the brand arises. The consumer feels affinities with the brand, feels that traits and features are shared among them, and that makes him feel special. During the first mandatory lockdown because of the Covid-19 pandemic, many brands worldwide reacted by attempting to satisfy the new needs of their consumers and fans, being information, reassurance, entertainment, or social connectedness. Whenever consumers felt that brands cared about them, they were grateful, and this connection was a step towards those brands becoming love brands because they were meaningful for them at a particular difficult time. Finally, Roberts (2005) claims that mystery is also necessary to arouse love. In order to keep consumers engaged, a brand must offer something new to uncover, a brand must surprise, and a brand must go beyond what is expected.

Building brand equity, arousing brand love, or becoming a lovemark, these are all alternative ways of making your brand stand out and matter. However, it is easier said than done, as it is an ongoing and everlasting work, which must be done every day and still exceed expectations and surprise. Does your brand have what it takes? What is the best way of being a "good" brand?

5.3   Being a social brand

The concept of "social brand" emerged as result of my experience as coordinator of a post-graduation course on branding and social media (post-graduate course on "Social Brands – Communication and Marketing in the Digital Environment"), a course that was pioneer in Portugal when it was launched in 2010. In addition, it also results from the scientific research that has been developed by me and all the teaching staff of the course on the topic. Another contribution comes from my experience, and of all the teaching staff, in advising our students in the development of branding plans applied to real cases. Thus, the notion of "social brands" has been brewing in our brains for the last 12 years, and we have been researching about it, collecting case studies, and deepening our knowledge about the most important dimensions of a social brand and how to nurture them.

When we launched this course in 2010, it was named post-graduate course on "Communication on Social Media". However, we soon realized that we were also addressing mobile marketing, user experience applied to websites and particularly ecommerce, the application of digital technologies to physical stores, and many other topics that were related to digital technologies in a broader sense. So, in 2012, I decided to organize a brainstorming workshop with all the teaching staff, to come up with a name for the course that expressed more accurately what students could find in our syllabus. During this workshop, we realized that we were focusing on the digital environment, but this is so intertwined with our physical existence, that it no longer made sense to think about these two dimensions separately, as we currently live onlife (Floridi, 2015). In addition, we realized that our focus was helping brands cope with the contemporary environment and become the best version of themselves possible. So, our course was more about brands than it was about social media.

And what were we teaching about how a brand can become "good" in such a volatile, complex, dynamic, and challenging digital environment? Well, a brand needs to be present in the digital environment and adapt to its nature. Companies were used to communicate in a one-direction and one-to-many paradigm, in which they pushed their message onto generally passive targets through mass media. Social media were radically disruptive and imposed a new paradigm, in which communication is multi-directional and many-to-many. Social media are a space for dialogue and conversation. If brands want to populate this space in a meaningful way, they must shift their communication paradigm to dialogue (Holtzhausen & Zerfass, 2013). So, brands need to learn how to be **social**. However, the digital environment is already overcrowded with brands, and contemporary customers are naturally disloyal, armed with digital tools that enable them to find the best bargains. Research had been pointing to the importance of brands building emotional bonds with consumers and fans that led to preference and, ultimately, to loyalty (Newlin, 2009). According to Kotler et al. (2017), the deepest connections between brands and consumers are grounded on shared values. Thus, brands must incorporate such values in their communication and action, and the values that spur more identification are the ones that aim at common good. So, brands also need to learn how to be **socially responsible**.

Thus, the "social" in social brands has this double sense of referring to sociability and to social responsibility. And how exactly can brands work on developing each of these dimensions?

As the concept of brand love is inspired in love applied to the relationship between humans, brand sociability can also be inspired by human sociability. And the grounding for human sociability is **empathy**. Brands can start this process by being emphatic, that is, by getting to know their target(s) at the deepest level possible and being able to put themselves in the shoes of their customers and fans. In fact, Turkle (2017) argues that empathy is the most essential of all human traits, and it is the one characteristic that makes us human. Brands must become the first and fiercest advocates of their customers' and fans' well-being and interests. This empathy will reflect positively on their sociability, as emphatic brands are open to listening and are genuinely interested in the perspectives of others, instead of being focused on spreading their own message. Empathic brands know how to engage in dialogue and are, therefore, naturally sociable. In addition, considering that social media emerged to connect people with people, if brands want to be present in this environment in a meaningful way for their target(s), they must become **humanized**, to be able to build and nurture the same kind of connection that people are seeking there. Personality was already a component of brands, a trait that they used to generate identification on the part of customers and fans, to build bonds. Brands can undergo the deepest process of humanization than merely developing and expressing a personality. Brands can develop their own personas and incorporate personality traits, behavioral quirks, a unique communication style, a particular sense of humor. The more a brand resembles a person and acts and reacts as a person, the more other persons will be able to connect to it. Social media have become central in the contemporary digital environment (Jenkins, 2006), and they are currently algorithmic, which means that they play an important role in shaping the reach, the engagement, and the influence of each content creator (van Dijck, Poell & de Waal, 2018). To succeed in this digital environment, empathic and humanized brands must be **sociable**, they have to be magnetic, as that special friend that everyone opens up to and who is always the life of the party. A sociable brand is good at listening and sensing the pulse of its community. It engages in true dialogue, instead of just pushing its own content. It answers to comments and questions and is able to spur engagement and participation with strategic calls to action. It knows how important it is to be grateful to consumers and fans for their attention, time, and support. It joins trends, it stars its own trends, and it builds a strong sense of community while making each member feel special. There are two communication techniques that research singles out as particularly useful for these purposes: storytelling and gamification. Storytelling is the core of content marketing, while gamification is frequently used in online community management. Storytelling appeals to the human brain, shaped by thousands of years of evolution in which the predominant way of communicating and preserving knowledge and culture was orality. Plus, storytelling is engaging because the audience is curious about how the narrative is going to unfold. The best stories are about values, thus enhancing identification and bonding between brands and consumers or fans (Pulizzi, 2012). Gamification also appeals to the primordial instinct of being the strongest, the fastest, the brightest, or simply the best to survive. But in online community management, elements of competition are applied to promote collaboration and to enhance the sense of belonging (Moise, 2013).

Turning to social responsibility now, this concept is based on the assumption that all organizations have the responsibility of contributing to the welfare of its community (Adi, Grigori & Crowther, 2015). This notion of community can be understood as the close circle that constitutes its direct environment – consumers and fans, business partners, competitors, geography – or it can be thought in a broader sense, as the planet itself. As the strongest bonds between brands and consumers or fans are rooted in an identification based on shared values, organizations should incorporate such values in their quotidian action. Living in a world where fake news, disinformation, and misinformation proliferate, contemporary consumers have become particularly suspicious and keen at scrutinizing and fact checking (Ceron et al., 2021). As consumers are increasingly interested in sustainability, many companies have been engaging in greenwashing, practices that aim to project an image of sustainability that does not correspond to the truth or that is only partially truthful (de Freitas Netto et al., 2020). Customers are demanding transparency from organizations, but they reward transparent organizations with their goodwill, preference, and, often, loyalty. Thus, it is very important that brands engage with causes that are consistent with their values. The concept of social responsibility is more associated with **solidarity**, but there are some broader formations that also include environmental responsibility or **sustainability** (Moody & Achebaum, 2014). As our planet faces such great challenges, many researchers and professionals are arguing that, from an ethical perspective, sustainability is more of an obligation than a possibility. In fact, trying to be more sustainable is, in fact, a matter of survival, of ensuring a survivable future, and that is what customers are demanding of organizations. Thus, social brands are socially responsible in what concerns both solidarity and sustainability, always in alignment with the values that are embedded in brand identity. Plus, it is also important that brands go beyond communication, or social marketing strategies that, while helping a certain cause by donating a percentage of profits, are at the same time and primordially trying to increase their own sales, and take action. Consumers respect, connect with, and ultimately become the biggest advocates of brands that are truly **activists**, instead of opportunists or slacktivists. Truly activists consistently work on the same causes, causes that are consistent with their values, and make altruistic contributions that are not connected to sales (but often have very positive impact on awareness, reputation, and brand love).

What do brands have to gain in becoming, and being, a social brand? Empathic, humanized, and sociable brands stand out, even in an accelerated, complex, fluid, and ephemeral platformized and datafied digital environment. In addition, brands that are activists of solidarity and sustainability causes are perceived by consumers and fans as brands that matter, because they have a clear positive impact on their community (closer or broader). Thus, brands that are both social and socially responsible are inspiring, approachable, and relatable but at the same time outstanding in their contribution to the common good. Consumers and brands connect with inspiring brands because they propose a future that they want to live in, and such brands invite them to become a part of such purpose. Social brands are lovable and deliver value both to companies and to consumers or fans.

References

Aaker, D. (1991). *Managing brand equity: Capitalizing on the value of a brand name.* New York: Free Press.

Aaker, D. (1996). *Building strong brands.* New York: Free Press.

Aaker, D. (2020). *Aaker on branding: 20 principles that drive success.* New York: Morgan James Publishing.

Adi, A., Grigori, G., & Crowther, D. (2015). *Corporate social responsibility in the digital age.* Cambridge: Emerald Insights.

Bauman, Z. (2000). *Liquid modernity.* London: Polity Press.

Carroll, B., & Ahuvia, A. (2005). Some antecedents and outcomes of brand love. *Marketing Letters, 17,* 79–89. https://doi.org/10.1007/s11002-006-4219-2

Castells, M. (1996). *The rise of the network society – The information age: Economy, society and culture* (vol. 1). Wiley-Blackwell.

Ceron, W., Lima-Santos, M.-F., & Quiles, M. (2021). Fake news agenda in the era of Covid-19: Identifying trends through fact-checking content. *Online Social Networks and Media, 21.* https://doi.org/10.1016/j.osnem.2020.100116

Davenport, T., & Beck, J. (2001). *The attention economy: Understanding the new currency of business.* Harvard: Harvard Business Review Press.

de Chernatony, L., & Christodoulides, G. (2004). Taking the brand promise online: Challenges and Opportunities. *Journal of Direct Data in Digital Marketing Practices - Interactive Marketing, 5,* 238–251. https://doi.org/10.1057/palgrave.im.4340241

de Freitas Netto, S. V., Sobral, M. F. F., Ribeiro, A. R. B., & Soares, G. R. L. (2020). Concepts and forms of greenwashing: A systematic review. *Environmental Sciences Europe, 32*(19). https://doi.org/10.1186/s12302-020-0300-3

Floridi, L. (2015). *The Onlife manifesto: Being human in a hyperconnected era.* New York: Springer. https://doi.org/10.1007/978-3-319-04093-6

Giddens, A. (1986). *The constitution of society: Outline of the theory of structuration.* Oakland: University of California Press.

Heep, A., Hjavard, S., & Lundby, K. (2015). Mediatization: Theorizing the interplay between media, culture and society. *Media, Culture & Society, 37*(2), 314–324. https://doi.org/10.1177/01634437155738

Holtzhausen, D., & Zerfass, A. (2013). Strategic communication: Pillars and perspectives of an alternative paradigm. In K. Sriramesh, A. Zerfass & J.-N. Kim (Eds.), *Public relations and communication management: current trends and emerging topics.* London: Routledge.

Jenkins, H. (2006). *Convergence culture: Where old and new media collide.* New York: New York University Press.

Kornberger, M. (2010). *Brand society: How brands transform society and lifestyle.* Cambridge: Cambridge University Press.

Kotler, P., Kartajaya, H., & Setiawan, I. (2017). *Marketing 4.0: Moving from traditional to digital.* London: Wiley.

Mamina, R., & Tolstikova, I. (2020). Phygital generation in free global communication. *International Journal of Open Information Technologies, 8*(1). https://bit.ly/3TpZhr5

Moise, D. (2013). Gamification: The new game in marketing. *Romanian Journal of Marketing, 2,* 22–33.

Moody, H. R., & Achebaum, W. A. (2014). Solidarity, sustainability, stewardship: Ethics across generations. *Interpretation, 68*(2), 150–158. https://doi.org/10.1177/0020964313517656

Newlin, K. (2009). *Passion brands.* New York: Prometheus Books.

Pappu, R., Quester, P., & Cooksey, R. (2005). Consumer-based brand equity: Improving the measurement – Empirical evidence. *Journal of Product and Brand Management, 14*(3), 143–154. https://doi.org/10.1108/10610420510601012

Pulizzi, J. (2012). The rise of storytelling as the new marketing. *Publishing Research Quarterly, 28,* 116–123. https://doi.org/10.1007/s12109-012-9264-5

Roberts, K. (2005). *Lovemarks: The future beyond brands.* New York: Powerhouse Books.

Turkle, S. (2017). *Alone together: Why we expect more from technology and less from each other.* London: Basic Books.

van Bommel, E., Edelman, D., & Ungerman, K. (2014). *Digitizing the consumer decision journey.* McKinsey & Company. https://bit.ly/3yMqxYT

Van Dijck, J., Poell, T., & de Waal, M. (2018). *The platform society: Public values in a connective world.* Oxford: Oxford University Press.

Conclusion

Brands have always taken products and services beyond themselves. Throughout the times, brands have developed and evolved, adding an infinite amount of complementary layers to products and services; ensuring their provenance and quality; telling the story of how they came to be and becoming the building blocks of the many stories that consumers can create; associating products and services with moments, aromas, memories, emotions, experiences, and aspirations; and endowing them with an identity, a personality, a sense of humor, a lifestyle, and a social status.

Brands are, in their essence, connectors. They are connectors between the creators, makers, and providers of products and services and those who experience them, enjoy them, and appropriate them. They are connectors between what is and the promise of what can be, extending desires and aspirations about achievement, happiness, and self-fulfillment. They are connectors between people with similar tastes and dreams, who strongly believe that there is more to life than making decision choices based on the best quality-price ratio.

Covid-19 was an unprecedented global event that radically changed the way we think and live, even if we are all trying to resume a post-pandemic quotidian. The threat of a deadly disease, the deprivation of our freedom during mandatory lockdown periods, the lack of small touches, warm smiles, and trivial words that we all took for granted led to a profound reflection and questioning about the way we live our lives.

Some brands found diverse ways of being meaningful during the most difficult times. Some changed their production and used the means at their disposal to contribute to society by producing scarce and much needed good, such as sanitizing gel or masks. Others drove solidary actions and mobilized their customers and fans, supporting health professionals, those who had lost their livelihood or those who were ill. Others yet simple kept us company and tried their best to entertain us and give us hope while we were locked up in our homes, missing our past and uncertain about our future. People bonded with these brands who were present at a time of difficulty and need.

DOI: 10.4324/9781003382331-7

As our daily lives resumed, our relationship with brands cannot go back to the way it was.

With a background of abundance and hyperconsumption (Lipovetsky, 2010), we experienced lack and scarcity. Used to touching screens and getting immediate response from our digital devices, we experienced impotence and we were obliged to wait. We also witnessed how our planet changed – for the better – when we slowed down. We started wondering about what we really need, how much, and how frequently. Struggling between the desire to travel again, to socialize more with friends and family, and to indulge in experiences and pleasures that were inaccessible during that period and the realization our consumption habits could change and that could lead to a more sustainable and healthier living, for each one and for the community, we started questioning consumption-stimulating discourses that marketing and advertising have been directing to us for decades. Maybe we do not need to follow the latest trend in fashion, maybe our eating habits are not the healthiest, maybe we shouldn't aspire so much to the perfect-filtered lives of others that we follow on social media, maybe it is not such a good deal buying something on a black-Friday deal that we don't really need. This questioning led us to holding brands accountable for creating and disseminating these discourses, for fueling consumption. This questioning led us to demanding from brands what marketing has been claiming for decades that they offer – win-win offers.

The post-pandemic consumer has maintained some habits, changed others, and acquired new ones. A new influence factor has emerged in the post-pandemic consumer journey – the demand for an honest and fair deal. Consumers are aware that doing business in our society holds many challenges. As they struggle to become more sustainable and solidary themselves and often fail, they have learned to respect and value brands that are undergoing the same journey. They reward brands that are committed to making a positive contribution to the world that present offers that are obviously beneficial not only for their business but also for consumers and for society in general.

This book presents an overview of the changes, both in consumer behavior and in brand management, that have emerged in this post-pandemic context. Drawing on the criteria that consumers are currently following to navigate their consumer journeys, we conceptualized the features that a brand needs to entail to stand out from others, to connect with consumers, and to matter to them. Such brands are **social** brands, in the double sense of being **sociable** and **socially responsible**. In order to become sociable, a brand built its identity as if it was a person, thus becoming **humanized**. Armed with a personality, a sense of humor, a communication style, emotions, and, above all, values, a brand can become **empathic**, thus being able to foster and nurture deep connections with consumers. Social responsibility entails both **sustainability** and **solidarity**. And communication is not enough. Consumers are demanding from brands that they take action in standing up and fighting for the causes that matter. In addition, this action must be fully transparent and aligned with the values that are core to the brand. Consumers respect and support **activist** brands that make a positive impact in the world, and not opportunistic brands that join movements and copy trending hashtags. Building a strong brand, that encompasses all these features, is not easy. In some respects, it may even be contradictory to some principles of marketing. Social brands don't sell much, they sell better. Maybe they don't grow every year because they have reached a sustainable balance based on loyalty. To become a social brand, it is necessary stepping out of the classical ever-growing capitalist model and finding new economic concepts and solutions. It is not brands on one side of the barricade, and consumers on the other, anymore. Sellers are buyers and buyers can be sellers, and we all need to collaborate to build a better future, for ourselves and for others to come. We hope this book inspires you, professional and/or consumer, to join this collaborative approach and to share our vision of a future that can be happier.

Index

Note: **Bold** page numbers refer to tables.

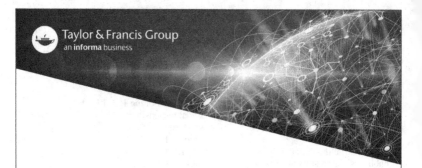

Printed in the United States
by Baker & Taylor Publisher Services